FIFTY TUNES

COMPOSED AND SET TO MUSIC

TARAVATI

A TALE

AND

THE

TWENTY-TWO MUSICAL SRUTIS

OF THE

HINDUS

FIFTY TUNES

COMPOSED AND SET TO MUSIC

TARAVATI

A TALE

AND

THE

TWENTY-TWO MUSICAL SRUTIS

OF THE

HINDUS

SOURINDRO MOHUN TAGORE

GYAN

Published by

GYAN

Gyan Publishing House
5, Ansari Road
Daryaganj, New Delhi-110002
Phone: 011-47034999, 9811692060
E-mail: books@gyanbooks.com

Distribution Network
gyanbooks.com
India, USA, Canada, UK, Australia

ISBN: 978-93-6920-426-7 (HB)

First Published, 1878

2nd Impression 2025

Printed at: Gyan Press, Delhi.

FIFTY TUNES COMPOSED AND SET TO MUSIC, TARAVATI A TALE AND THE TWENTY-TWO MUSICAL SRUTIS OF THE HINDUS
Author: SOURINDRO MOHUN TAGORE

FIFTY TUNES,

COMPOSED AND SET TO MUSIC,

BY

SOURINDRO MOHUN TAGORE, Mus. Doc.,

Founder and President of the Bengal Music School,

&c., &c., &c.

1878.

To

THE HON'BLE SIR ASHLEY EDEN,

K. C. S. I.,

Lieutenant-Governor of Bengal,

THIS BOOK

IS

MOST RESPECTFULLY DEDICATED

BY

HIS MOST GRATEFUL

AND

OBLIGED SERVANT,

THE AUTHOR.

CONTENTS.

CONTENTS.

PREFACE.

THE following pages give, in a collected form, some of the tunes which the author has composed on different occasions. In setting them, (at the express wish of some of his European friends,) to the European system of notation and in attempting to adapt them for the *Piano* or other foreign instruments, he has been obliged to make alterations in some of the pieces, whereby they have, to a certain extent, been divested of the variety of embellishments which are so characteristic of Hindu Music.

FIFTY TUNES.

RÁGIṆÍ BHÚPA-KALYÁṆA.

TÁLA MADHYAMÁNA.

---

* Words by the HON'BLE MAHARAJAH JOTEENDRO MOHUN TAGORE, BAHADOOR, composed for the occasion of the reception given by the natives to H. R. H. THE PRINCE OF WALES, on his visit to Calcutta, and sung before him.

Though hum- ble our re- cep- tion be, And though
our strains may hal- ting run, The — lo- yal
heart we bring to thee, Is war- mer than our Eas-
tern — sun.

(1.)

RÁGI<u>N</u>Í BHÚPÁLÍ.

TÁLA MADHYAMÁNA.

First Strain.

Second Strain.

(2.)

RÁGIṈÍ ARUṈA-MALLÁRA.

TÁLA DRUTA-TRITÁLÍ.

(3.)

RÁGIṈÍ SURATA.

TÁLA MADHYAMÁNA.

(4.)

RÁGINÍ BHÚPÁLÍ.

TÁLA DRUTA-TRITÁLÍ.

(5.)

RÁGINÍ BIBHÁSA.

TÁLA SURPHÁKTÁ.

(6.)

RÁGIN̲I SÁRAÑGA.

TÁLA EKATÁLA.

First Strain.

Second Strain.

(7.)

RÁGIṈÍ BEHÁGA.

TÁLA MADHYAMÁNA.

(8.)

RÁGINÍ IMAN-KALYÁNA.

TÁLA DRUTA-TRITÁLÍ.

(9.)

RÁGINÍ ŚYÁMA.

TÁLA PÁT-TAL.

(10.)

RÁGIṈÍ HÁMIRA.

TÁLA MADHYAMÁNA.

(11.)

RÁGIṈÍ KHÁMBÁJA.

TÁLA MADHYAMÁNA.

(12.)

RÁGIṈÍ BEHÁGA.

Tála Madhyamána.

(13.)

RÁGINÍ CHHÁYÁ-NATA.

TÁLA MADHYAMÁNA.

(14.)

RÁGIṈÍ KEDÁRÁ.

TÁLA MADHYAMÁNA.

(15.)

RÁGIN̲Í IMAN-KALYÁN̲A.

TÁLA MADHYAMÁNA.

(16.)

RÁGIṈÍ BHÚPÁLÍ.

TÁLA MADHYAMÁNA.

(17.)

RÁGINÍ GAURA-SÁRAÑGA.

TÁLA MADHYAMÁNA.

(18.)

RÁGINÍ GAURA-SÁRAÑGA.

TÁLA MADHYAMÁNA.

(19.)

RÁGINÍ BIBHÁSHA.

TÁLA MADHYAMÁNA.

(20.)

RÁGINÍ IMAN.

TÁLA MADHYAMÁNA.

(21.)

RÁGIN̲Í SOHINI.

TÁLA THUÑRÍ.

(22.)

RÁGIṈÍ MEGHA.

TÁLA MADHYAMÁNA.

(23.)

RÁGIṈÍ JHIJHITI.

TÁLA THUṄRÍ.

(24.)

RÁGIṆÍ IMAN-KALYÁṆA.

TÁLA MADHYAMÁNA.

First Strain.

Second Strain.

(25.)

RÁGIṈÍ SÁRAÑGA.

TÁLA MADHYAMÁNA.

(26.)

RÁGINÍ LUM-JHIJHIT.

TÁLA MADHYAMÁNA.

(27.)

RÁGINÍ YOGINÁ.

TÁLA THUÑRÍ.

(28.)

RÁGINÍ BIBHÁSHA.

TÁLA MADHYAMÁNA.

(29.)

RÁGIṈÍ BIBHÁSHA.

TÁLA PAT-TÁL.

(30.)

RÁGINÍ CHHÁYÁNATA.

TÁLA MADHYAMÁNA.

(31.)

RÁGINÍ KEDÁRÁ.

TÁLA MADHYAMÁNA.

(32.)

RÁGA NATA-NÁRÁYANA.

TÁLA MADHYAMÁNA.

(33.)

RÁGINI SÁRAÑGA.

TÁLA EKATÁLA.

(34.)

RÁGIN̲Í PURABÍ.

TÁLA MADHYAMÁNA.

(35.)

RÁGIṈÍ JAÑGALÁ-SÁRAÑGA.

TÁLA MADHYAMÁNA.

(36.)

RÁGINÍ IMAN-PURIYÁ.

TÁLA MADHYAMÁNA.

(37.)

RÁGINÍ BEHÁGA.

TÁLA CHAUTÁLA.

(38.)

RÁGIṈÍ SÁRAÑGA.

TÁLA EKATÁLA.

(39.)

RÁGINÍ JAÑGALÁ-SURATA.

TÁLA CHAUTÁLA.

(40.)

RÁGIṈÍ YOGIṈÁ.

TÁLA MADHYAMÁNA.

First Strain.

Second Strain.

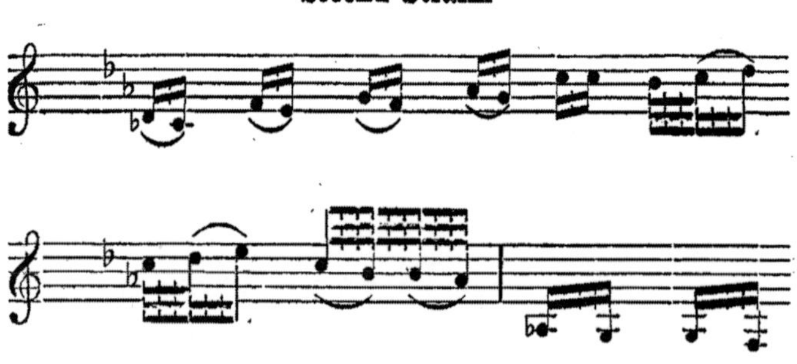

(41.)

RÁGINÍ MÁLAŚRÍ.

TÁLA DRUTA-TRITÁLÍ.

(42.)

RÁGIN̲Í SURAṬA.

TÁLA DRUTA-TRITÁLÍ.

(43.)

RÁGINÍ BIBHÁSHA.

TÁLA CHUATÁLA.

(44.)

RÁGI<u>N</u>Í BEHÁGA.

TÁLA CHAUTÁLA.

(45.)

RÁGIṈÍ BEHÁGA.

TÁLA MADHYAMÁNA.

(46.)

RÁGINÍ BHAIRABI.

TÁLA MADHYAMÁNA.

(47.)

RÁGINÍ BIBHÁSHA.

TÁLA MADHYAMÁNA.

(48.)

RÁGIṈÍ HÁMBIRA.

TÁLA MADHYAMÁNA.

(49.)

RÁGINÍ MÁLIGAURÁ.

TÁLA CHAUTÁLA.

(50.)

RÁGIṈÍ KARNÁTÍ.

TÁLA MADHYAMÁNA.

GOD SAVE THE QUEEN.

RÁGINÍ BIBHÁSHA.

TÁLA CHAUTÁLA.

APPENDIX.

The following are the *first* two airs, composed about 20 years ago, by the Hon'ble Maharajah Joteendro Mohun Tagore, Bahadoor, for the native orchestra, *first* organized by him:—

A

RÁGIṈÍ JHIJHIT.

Tála Madhyamána.

B

RÁGIN̲Í KHÁMBÁBATÍ.

TÁLA MADHYAMÁNA.

TÁRÁVATÍ:

A TALE,

TRANSLATED INTO ENGLISH.

BY

RAJAH COMM. SOURINDRO MOHUN TAGORE,

MUS. DOC., C. I. E., &c., &c., &c.

Calcutta:

PRINTED BY I. C. BOSE & CO., STANHOPE PRESS, 249, BOW-BAZAR STREET, AND PUBLISHED BY THE AUTHOR.

1881.

PREFACE.

Years ago the following legendary tale was written by my revered mother. From motives of filial piety, I undertook the translation of the work; and now present the reader with the following pages.

TÁRÁVATÍ.

A TALE.

ON the east of India lay the extensive kingdom of Magadha. In it lived a very wealthy man, named Dayásindhu, a spice merchant. In consideration of his immense wealth, he also went by the name of Dhanapati, or the lord of wealth. He had a wife divinely beautiful and crowned with every virtue. Her name was Táràvatí. The merchant and his consort pined for want of a son, for which they unceasingly prayed to God in heaviness of heart, and celebrated many religious ceremonies. Of a night, as Táràvatí lay alone on a fresh bed, after having, during the day, observed the *Astamí Vrata** and worshipped Chandíká, she dreamt that a surpassingly beautiful girl of eight, decked from head to foot, and wearing a piece of red silk cloth, sat on Táràvatí's bed, and with a smiling countenance and in mellow tones, addressed the sleeping fair one thus, "Táràvatí! thou art a virtuous lady. I am well pleased with thy devotions. Listen to me! Go to the *as'vattha* tree, which stands on the east of the village. On the north-eastern side of it, under about two yards of ground, thou wilt find a pot made of eight

* This religious ceremony is celebrated by Hindu females on the eighth day of the lunar fortuight.

metals, and an image of the Lion-riding goddess.* Before the day breaks, go to the place, with thy husband, and unearthing the pot and the image, take them out. Then raising a large temple on the site, establish the image in it, and worship it with all the sanctimonious rites. By this means, thou wilt soon be blest with a son, bearing all the marks of future greatness, as well as with a daughter, graced with every virtue." Filled with delight at this dream, as Tárávatí stretched out her arms to hug in the damsel to her bosom, she smiled and was no more. Tárávatí awoke. She looked around, but saw nothing. She was then lost in thought, when lo! a divine voice said, "Tárávatí! tarry no more. Up and go to the place with thy husband. At break of day, it will be filled with people." Hearing this extra-mundane sound, she hied to the couch of her lord, and seeing him asleep, thought, that to awaken him was wrong; but then the divine behest must be obeyed. She decided for the latter. Thinking this, as she laid her hand upon the feet of Dayásindhu, he awoke, and rising up, said to his wife, "My love, is it morning?" Tárávatí said, "Light of my eye, it is hardly day—it is near day-break. Love, I have dreamt a wonderful dream to-night, and heard a divine voice, which I have hastened here to tell you." Dayásindhu became curious. Tárávatí related all. Having heard it, her husband said, "My love, you are perfection itself;

* Durgá—the consort of Siva and personification of the cosmic force—rides on a lion.

and I am blest with the possession of such a treasure!" Then Dayásindhu and his wife, accompanied with their servants, went to the *as'vattha* tree. The merchant-prince sang a hymn in praise of Mahámáyá, and directed his men to dig the ground for about two yards. They fell to digging the place, until they came to the pot composed of eight metals. Dhanapati took it up reverentially with his own hands, and gave it to his partner. Táráváti placed it on her head, and stood there. Then Dhanapati took up the image of the Lion-riding goddess. Táráváti placed the pot before the goddess and bowed down to the deity, with her husband. They then went back to their house, to bring the necessary things, for worship. It waxed late, and folks began to gather round the place where the goddess was found, and there was noise and bustle. The merchant pitched a camp on a cleaned spot and established the image in it. The people of the village and the friends and acquaintances of Dhanapati extolled him and bestirred themselves to bring the priest and to procure the necessary things, such as flowers. In time the people came with the family priest and other Brahmins versed in the Vedas, as well as with the necessary articles. The merchant welcomed the Brahmins and spread cushions for them. They sat down and applauded and blessed him. Dhanapati in all humility paid his reverence to the Brahmins and said, "Sires, favor me with worshipping the goddess, in due form." "Very well, sir," returned they, and set about the business. Táráváti now came there in a palankeen, guarded by a body of men. When the Brahmins had done, Táráyatí and her husband were engaged in worshipping and hymning the image. When they had finished their devotions, they fed the Brahmins sumptuously, and gave them *dakhinás ;** then they fed the poor people. After having discharged every duty, Dhanapati returned to his palace with his wife. Afterwards, he erected an alabaster temple for the goddess, with a threatre and a garden and tank adjoining, the last being furnished with four sets of stairs. The place gradually became a place of trade, and people flocked there, to pray the image, for having their desires. The place thus obtained the name of Chandítalá.

After some time, through the blessings of Chandíká, Táráyatí was with child. When it was full ten months, Táráyatí fell in throes and gave birth to a son and a daughter bearing all the auspicious marks. Dhanapati now considered himself the happiest of men and distributed money and alms to Brahmins and the poor. When the time for *Annaprásana*† came, he celebrated the ceremony and named the twins, Srimanta and Ketakí, the former for the male, the latter for the female child. In time, Srimanta shone out like the summer sun in his meridian

---

* After feeding the Brahmin, the host gives him a small amount of money—generally a silver piece, which may be looked upon as the price of the condescension on the part of that prime of men.

† When the child is six months old, the parents celebrate a religious ceremony, on the occasion of which, it first tastes rice and receives a name.

glory, and the daughter beamed like the autumnal moon. And this made the hearts of their parents glad. In a short time the boy and the girl became proficient in many sciences and arts. Hearing the praises of Srimanta and Ketakí, match-makers* from various countries began to flock into Magadha. Dhanapati married with great pomp and splendour his son to the daughter of Vadra Sen, Raja of Rámnagar, and his daughter, to Rámnáth, son of Sankara Dutt of Rájnagar. The marriage of Ketakí was celebrated the day following that of the marriage of Srimanta. Dhanapati kept his son-in-law at his own residence. When Srimanta and Rámnáth came of age, he initiated them into the mysteries of his profession, and said, "I will reward each of you according to his deserts, in his line." Encouraged by their governor, both the young men shone in business, and riches began to pour into the treasury. Gratified with their success, Dhanapati gave each of them a precious diamond ring. The young people were delighted, and addressed themselves to their duties with increased vigour.

Of a certain night in summer, Srimanta woke during the small hours and said to Rámnáth, "Ho Rám! I am very much oppressed with heat. Let us walk out into the garden and refresh ourselves with the cool breeze blowing over the tank." They thereupon came to the place, and began to eye the beauty of the garden. The moon was beaming mild;

* The Hindus have a class of professional match-makers.

the fish were gliding in rows by the bank; the vernal gale was blowing on all sides, laden with fragrance from the blooming blossoms; the cuckoo was pouring forth its throat melodiously; various trees in rows beautified the grove; the night-birds were screaming over ripe juicy fruits, the stones of which dropped to the bottom of the trees. The east gradually began to blush and brighten—the luminary of night was about to 'hide his diminished head.' Seeing all this, Rámnáth said to his companion, "See! see! my friend, how the Moon is dancing in the liquid mirror!" Srimanta replied, "Nay, not so; the Moon is agitated for grief of Kumudiní, who has veiled herself, seeing that her beloved was about to depart."*

They were talking thus, when a stalwart ascetic appeared before them with a smile. The personage had long whiskers, his hair was matted and hung down behind his head. His body was covered with ashes, he had a *rudráksha* rosary on his neck, and he bore a trident in his hand. Srimanta rose up, paid his reverence to the holy man, and stood before him. The ascetic blessed Srimanta and asked, "Srimanta, can you recognise me now?" The young man replied, "I think I have seen you somewhere, sir; I don't remember it clearly." "Nandíkeswar,"† rejoined the figure, "has sent me here, to bring you

---

* It is a classical conceit that the Kumudiní or water-lily, is the spouse of the Moon; as the Kamaliní or lotus is that of the Sun.

† An attendant of Siva.

in mind of your former life. Hark!" Saying this, he narrated all the facts in detail, and gave a flute to Srimanta. "Hie you to the Sandal wood, and deliver Promodiní." The ascetic said this and vanished. When the holy man had disappeared, the mind of Srimanta became highly agitated. He said to his companion, "My friend, bear tidings of my leaving my home, for a distant country, to my dear parents. Farewell!" "It is not proper for you to go to a distant land alone, leaving me behind," replied his companion. "I shall be able to help you in time of trouble, if I be by you. I shall therefore join you." Youth is the season of curiosity; but seeing the eagerness of Rámnáth, Srimanta said, "If both of us were to go, we should acquaint father of this, by letter, and then go away privately." Having determined on this, they gave a letter to a warder of their house and departed. When the man delivered the note to Dhanapati, he read it and hastened with the tidings to his wife. On hearing this, Tárávatí's eyes filled with tears; she said, "My love, at once despatch men in search of them. I shall go to the temple of the goddess and fast for three nights. Should good news reach in the meantime, I will live—else I will put an end to this existence." Dhanapati despatched men in different directions. Tárávatí became disconsolate for the absence of her son, and became engaged in prayers to the goddess.

On the other hand, Srimanta and Rámnáth travelled through various countries, and at last arrived at the country, called Udra where they spent a night at the house of the court pandit of Vijay Singha, prince of the place. Táráratí having fasted full three nights, the goddess was well pleased with her and said in an aerial voice, "Táráratí, fear not! Rise up. I am always protecting thy child. This day two weeks, thy Srimanta will come to thee, with his new bride and Rámnáth." Comforted thus, Táráratí rose up and paid her obeisance to the image. She then returned to her home with a cheerful heart, and related all to her husband. "No need of anxiety now!" said she, "let us prepare dress and ornaments for the bride." The merchant and his consort made the preparations, and remained expecting the pair.

When Srimanta and Rámnáth awoke at the house of the court pandit of Udra, they saw that the Moon was about to set and that the King of day was coming, 'rejoicing in the east.' The birds were tuning their throats. They rose, and after having finished their morning devotions, went in the direction of the Sandal wood. After proceeding some way, they met with some husbandmen, tilling the ground. The young men came up to them and asked, "My friends, how far is it to the Sandal wood?" Hearing this interrogatory, the men replied, "From what country do your honors come? And why do you enquire for the Sandal wood?" "We are bound for that wood," answered Srimanta. At this, a hoary-headed swain said, "So please your honors, listen to the mystery of the place. Formerly, there was a city, named

Uddípaní, by the forest, laved by the river Sálí. In it lived a wealthy merchant, named Priyamvada Sen. He had two wives. Priyamvada was a voluptuous person. One day, he was sporting with his second wife in the water, when a devotee faced him. The soft king was so intoxicated with the sport, that he did not break it even at the sight of the sage. Incensed at the complete self-abandonment of the king to Paphian pleasures, the holy man said, 'Wretch, darest thou slight me, because of thy wealth? For this, thy paramour shall live a bird in this wood. Thou shalt die on the instant; and this teeming city shall be a wilderness.' In virtue of this curse, Priyamvada met his end then and there, and his love was converted into a bird of the Sandal wood. Thereafter a tiger began to commit havoc on the inhabitants. Seeing this, the citizens began to desert the city. Since then, I have been living at this place, leaving Uddípaní. The wood is not far off. There is a mountain two miles distant. Ascending to the top of it, you will see the Sálí river. The forest on the other side is the forest you seek. Now it goes by the name of the Frightful forest. If any man chance to go there, he dies out of hand. Only the fishermen fish in the river. I have heard from their lips that no sound is heard of any living soul, save that a female bird sings on a bough of a tree on the river. Sirs, from your appearances, I ween that you come of respectable and rich parents. For some cause or other, you have come to a far country, in grief. I am a clown, and it ill beseems me to advise men like you. Still, I beseech you with clasped hands, not to go to the Sandal wood, by any means. Should you go there, slighting my warning, you will most probably lose your lives." "Never fear, friend," said Srimanta, "pray, show us the right way and tell us how to cross the river and come to the wood." The swain said, "Excuse me, but I look upon you as doomed. If you must go to that fatal place, that's the way. After passing the forest in front, you will come upon a mountain, ascending which, you will see the Sandal wood, on the other side of the river. Fishermen fish there in boats. They will ferry you over, for a trifle."

Agreeably to this direction, Srimanta crossed the forest in front and came to the mountain in question; whereupon his joy knew no bounds. He ascended the mountain, and found that what the husbandman had said, was true. But as the day had waxed late, the fishermen had gone home, after fishing. So the travellers were obliged to stay there for the night. "Now came still evening on"—Srimanta looked at the wished-for wood, and stayed in the mountain for the night. Rámnáth brought fruits; when the female bird began to sing thus:—

Song.

"My love—my love! where is he gone?
For him I pine a bird alone.
I've lost my love through Fortune's frown;
The Morrow brings my wronger down."

Srimanta was enraptured and astonished at this song, and said to his companion, "Hark! hark! my friend. You have never heard a bird sing more sweetly." So they both listened intently to the strains. When the bird ceased, Srimanta and Rámnáth fed on the fruits, and reposed in the mountain. When the day broke, the sun looked like a heap of Javá-flowers. The bird, seeing no signs of her beloved on the appointed day, began to think, "It is strange! Will the word even of the ascetic prove untrue, for my bad luck? Then, there is no use of dragging on this miserable life." Having determined on self-destruction, she perched on a vakul tree by the stream.

On the other hand, Srimanta and Rámnáth stood expecting a boat. When a boat came, Rámnáth went to the men and said, "Ho fishermen, we intend to cross the stream. Pray, ferry us over." Hearing this, the fishermen laughed and said, "From what country do you come, sirs? Don't you know that the entrance into the Sandal forest is death? We shan't be able to row you over." Saying this, they departed. Then Rámnáth said to an old fisherman, with misgivings, "Friend, do ferry us over, and you shall have a hundred coins." At this tempting offer, the Triton thought, "I have never seen one hundred coins together, in my life. I have not long to live; and this sum would maintain my wife and sons easily." The man consented. The young man delivered the money to the fisherman, and entering into the at, they were about to leave the shore, when the wife of the man appeared on the scene and ejaculated, "Halloa! what for are you bound for the Sandal wood? I have never given you one hard word. Why then are you bent on self-destruction? When you are gone, who would maintain us?" The woman began to weep and wail. "Carry home the sum," replied her husband, "which these gentlemen have given me. I will just ferry their honors over and return." At this, the woman said, "For this trifling sum, I shan't be able to risk your life. If they give a thousand coins, I shall fasten a rope to your boat, and sit in another, on this side of the stream. As soon as the gentlemen alight, I will pull your boat off the shore. If they agree to this, I can give my consent." Srimanta agreed, and taking out a diamond ring from his finger, gave it to the fisherwoman. She laughed at this, and said, "Is this your thousand coins. Why? This is a bit of glass. I don't require this." "Good wife," said her husband, "do not slight these gentlemen. This ring must be of high price—no doubt of that. I well know the value of this ring. Once on a time, such a gem belonging to our Prince had fallen into the water. I rescued it, and received a handsome reward for it. The minister said that the price of the ring was a thousand coins. This ring is not inferior to the other one. We shall get a thousand coins for it, if we sell it to a merchant." Then the fisherwoman tied a rope to her husband's boat, and sat in another, of larger dimensions. The fisherman launched his smaller skiff with Srimanta and Rámnáth. The female bird, in the meantime, had wept bitterly, and plunging in the tide, was trying to make away with herself, when she saw two boats appearing in the middle of the stream, one of which was comparatively large. Seeing this, she thought, "Perhaps the word of the prophet will prove true, after all. Let me see which way the boats take." Thereupon, she watched their course eagerly. When the smaller boat neared, she saw in it two young men, and an old boatman; in the other, and larger one, sat an old woman, holding fast a rope. When the skiff neared the shore, she saw a young person, resembling her paramour in form and features. "Ah!" exclaimed she, "will it again be given to me, to bless my eyes with the sight of that beloved countenance? O God! what more shall I suffer?" Looking steadfastly at the young man, she observed a mark on his person, and knew it to be certain that he was her own lost love, beyond the shadow of a doubt. She thought, "Let me now sit amidst the foliage, and see where they direct their steps." When the boat had well nigh reached the shore, the fisherwoman pulled the rope and cried, "For God's sake, do not go further near the shore. Tell them to go out on land. Should they not heed you, throw them into the water." "What, man?" exclaimed Rámnáth, "if we have to swim from here to the shore, we shall do it, after drowning both of you, husband and wife, with the boats." The fisherman trembled, and said, "Sirs, I havn't told you anything. Why then are you wroth with me? Pray, be at ease. I will anon land you on the shore." He immediately landed his skiff. Srimanta and Rámnáth jumped on land, and entered the forest. The fisherman, with his wife, went home.

On entering the wood, Srimanta said, "My friend, how beautiful are these trees bending beneath their weight of fruits. The fragrance of blowing flowers, mingling with the scent of the Sandal trees, is being perpetually wafted by the breeze, throughout the wood. Seeing all this, meseems this sylvan scene is the haunt of some god." Talking thus, they came to a tank, dejected at not finding the expected female bird. The air was eloquent with the hum of bees, feeding on liquid sweets from lotuses that bloomed on the breast of the tank. Viewing the scene, it appeared to Srimanta, as if all this were not new to him, as if he had seen the place before. Cogitating thus, he saw some pieces of red cloth, hanging from a Kadamva tree. On a stone at its bottom, were placed things necessary for ablution. At sight of these, the son of Dhanapati recollected the word of the ascetic. He thereupon began to play on the flute given by the holy sage. On hearing the sound, immediately the female bird descended from her perch, and sat on the shoulder of Srimanta. As the young man touched her with his hand for catching her, she fell to the ground, and lo! was converted into an exceedingly beautiful and shining lady, with flowing locks, wearing wet clothes; and in this form she stood before the astonished youth. Srimanta gazed steadfastly for a while, like a statue. He then recognized her, and addressing her, "My love!" hugged her to his bosom. Rámnáth was the very image of wonder. "What's this!" exclaimed he. "Did Párvatí live as a bird, for some purpose, to resume her proper form now?" The fair one, reposing on the breast of her charmer, thought, "Even as Rati found new life on the bosom of her restored lord, so have I, on that of my own dear love." She bathed her beloved with tears. "My soul," said her lover, "your tears are withering my bosom,—pray, do you cool it with the ambrosia of your speech."

The damsel was delighted with this speech of her lover, but she could not speak from shame. "I beseech you," went on Srimanta, "do you forgive all my faults." The lady opened her lips, "Soul of my soul, I am ashamed because of the presence of your companion." Srimanta said, "Dear, he is no other than my sister's husband. His name is Rámnáth. He is my best friend. But for his infinite pains on my behalf, it would have been hard for me to regain you. As he is nearly connected with me, you should leave off shame in his presence." Learning this, Pramodá was glad. Then Srimanta asked her, "My love, why are your clothes wet?" "Honey," returned the fair one, "have you forgotten the past? I will remind you of it. We had our home here. Not far from the forest, stands a beautiful brick-built mansion. We lived in it; and passed our days happily. We drank of the pure waters of this river—we sported in it. We knew no harm. Once, taking the necessary things, you came with me to bathe in this tank. You loosened my bound braid, and threw lotuses on my person, by way of dalliance. I drew you by main force, and splashed water and threw lotuses on your lovely person. Gradually we became lost to everything, save the consciousness of ecstacy in each other's embrace. At this point of time, came an ascetic stark naked, and stood on the bank, smiling at the sight of us. Suddenly my gaze fell on him. On seeing him, I hung down my head, and stood in the water mute and motionless. Seeing this alteration in my manner, you took my hand sadly and said, 'My dear love, of what fault have I been suddenly guilty, that you should be at once annoyed with me? If I have, pray, forgive me. Why has the eclipse of indignation darkened that moon of a countenance of yours. My mental light it darkens, dear. If you do not prove kind, I will die.' Touched at your plaintive appeal, I said bashfully, 'Lord, it is not displeasure that has changed me. Look at the cause. A shameless man stark naked, like any beast of the field or bird of the air, with a matted head of hair, is overlooking our sport and laughing. It is this which has made me hang down my head.' 'Where is that villain?' you exclaimed. 'Look there,' said I, 'he is standing there.' Seeing your wrath, and hearing the abuse you applied to him, he shook all over, and roared out, 'Abandoned wretch! you have dared slight me. Die, slave, for this!' No sooner had this curse escaped his lips, than my lord shook like an aspen leaf and fell down dead. The sage then eyed me and said, 'Since you have compared me profanely to the beasts and the fowls, you shall live in the Sandal wood as a bird.' I fell down at his feet and implored mercy. He relented and said with a smile, 'My word will not go for nothing. You will live in this state for some time; after which you shall leave the feathered form, and regain a human shape.' I then rejoined, 'Sire, how shall I meet again with my lord?' 'Your dead lord,' returned the sage, 'shall regain you in his next life.' I then enquired, 'Vouchsafe to inform me where he will take his birth, and how I shall regain him.' The anchoret remarked, 'Your husband shall be born as the son of Dayásindhu, the spice-merchant of Magadha. After he has completed his eighteenth year, he shall hear your tidings from an ascetic, and come in search of you.' 'Sire,' said I, 'how, in his next life, shall I be able to recognise him? And what if I could? Although I shall regain my human form, still I shall then be old, my husband will be a young man. Further, on account of his change of life, the hearts of both of us will alter. And, even if he took me back, I should suffer blame, for communion with a man to whom I was not joined in holy wedlock. So that, holy sage, your blessing is useless to me. I don't require your favor. Permit me to follow my lord. I don't wish to live.' At my lamentation, that best of ascetics said, 'Child, do not fear. Your husband shall appear before you in his present form, so that you will recognize him at once. When he comes to this forest, you shall sit on his shoulder; when he will touch you with his hand, you shall regain your present lovely form, and be blest in the enjoyment of your lord's company.' Saying this, he vanished. Lord, since then I have been living as a bird in this wood. I have been counting days. Through my good fortune, you have come here to-day and freed me from my feathered existence. I am now completely blest. But, love, let me ask of you one thing—What's the cause of your coming here? Did you remember the past?" "Beloved," replied Srimanta, "I have no other motive of coming here; it is only to regain you that I am here, after travelling many countries. I didn't remember an iota of the facts of my former life. I learned the facts relating to this Sandal wood from an ascetic, and have come here to regain you, and I have received you back." "Will you kindly satisfy my curiosity," asked the damsel, "by relating in detail what the ascetic told you?" Srimanta began, "A nude anchoret appeared before me and said, 'Ho youth, in former life you were the son of a wealthy Vaisya. Your name was Priyamvada. Your parents departed this life while you were yet a child. You were brought up by your maternal aunt, who educated you in various branches of learning, and married you to a girl, named Gandhinī. Gandhiní was not a very fair-looking girl, and was disliked by you. For this reason, after much search, your aunt married you for the second time to a girl named Pramodá. Having obtained Pramodá, you became exceedingly enamoured of her, and always remained at her side. One day, you went to sport in the waters with Pramodá, when a nude anchoret came there; and being slighted by you, cursed you in wrath. In virtue of this curse, you met your end. Then you have taken your birth as the son of Dhanapati.' After relating all this, he handed me a flute. He then added, 'Go to the Sandal wood, with this pipe. On hearing its notes, a female bird will alight on your shoulder. At the touch of your hand, she will leave off her bird-like form, and regain her own. You will thus regain your Pramodá.' Then the sage narrated what had befallen Gandhiní, and after this, vanished." Pramodá said, "My dearest love, if you do not feel weary, oblige me by detailing what befell Gandhiní." "I will," answered Srimanta, "tell you what I have heard from the hermit. When the ascetic I have told you of, had vanished, after having cursed us, Gandhiní came to the tank in search of us. On finding my dead body, and not finding you at all, she broke out into lamentations. Melted by her tears, the ascetic again appeared on the scene, and acquainted her with the calamity that had crushed us. Gandhiní fell at the feet of the hermit, and supplicated, 'Sire, I am helpless. As I am an ugly thing, I have never been beloved of my lord. Whenever my lord had expressed his dissatisfaction with me, I have never taken it to heart. I was always engaged in serving my lord. I have never looked with dissatisfaction on anything which my lord held dear. Since I could distinguish right from wrong, I have never looked on any other man with impure thoughts. Lord, I am perpetually wretched; for what sin have you inflicted on me the terrible penalty of widowhood? I am not conscious of any transgression towards you; do you, lord, grant my prayer that I may regain my lord in this life; or else, I will hang myself outright; and you shall bear on your head the sin of having killed a woman.' The sage complacently said, 'With whatever prayer you will resign your life at the junction of the Ganges with the ocean, shall be granted you in next life.' On hearing this, the girl took farewell of the ascetic, and going to the place to which she was directed, prayed that in her next state of existence she might be a surpassingly beautiful woman, remembering her former life, that she might regain her late husband, and that she might gain his affections. Praying thus, she gave up the ghost. Gandhiní was born as the daughter of Vadra Sen Ráy, of Rámnagar. Her name is Naliní. Lately I have wedded her. All this I have learnt from the ascetic."

On hearing this relation, Pramodá dropped down to the ground in a trance. Srimanta took her up in his lap and found that she was certainly dead. At this Srimanta began to cry. Rámnáth at once came up to him and asked, "Why do you weep, eh?" "Satisfy yourself as to the cause, with your own eyes," said his companion, "What shall I say?" Having heard the strange incidents, Rámnáth said, "Probably you have told her the history of Gandhiní. And her trance is owing to that." "Excuse me," cried Srimanta. "I see that my days are numbered here. You are my best of friends. Do you prepare without delay a funeral pyre. I will plunge into it and put a stop to all my miseries. Afterwards, go to my dear parents, and conveying my infinite reverence to their hallowed feet, say, 'Your Srimanta has bidden you an everlasting adieu, and has entered the funeral pyre.' Do you then console them. Let my dear sister be always at their side, so that their grief may be partially assuaged. Henceforth you are their only stay; pray see that they do not come to trouble. O God! is it to get this luckless wretch of a son that they fasted and prayed? I am a great sinner. It is for my sin in coming here without seeing them, that this has befallen me. O mother! O father! O my dear sister! I shall die without seeing you—I name you for the last time. Farewell!" Ramnath's eyes filled with tears at the lamentations of his friend. Unable to contain himself, he said, "Forbear, my friend. It ill becomes you to put an end to your life, for a bird. If you die, don't think that I will ever return to our country. I will put a question to you. Do you answer it, and do what you like." "Pray, out with it," said Srimanta. "I have not long to live, my voice is being choked." Rámnáth rejoined, "When we were coming to this place, the husbandmen and the fishermen told us that those who went to the Sandal forest never returned. This is about to be verified now. Probably this fatal bird destroys incomers, sometimes as a tigress, at others as a woman, at others again, as a female bird. Whatever it be, it ill beseems sensible men to abandon themselves to grief. Resigning all affection for the mother who has borne you for ten months in her womb, and for the father, who has brought you up with affection, you certainly deserve censure for this impatience. You should now return to your parents and make them happy." Srimanta fell down to the ground in a trance. Seeing this state of his friend, Rámnáth thought, "This is not so very bad, after all. At this opportunity, I will burn the body of this syren; and then, consoling Srimanta for what is past and buried, take him home to his house." Thinking thus, he prepared a pyre, and no sooner had he thrown the corpse in it, than Padmávatí, the maid of the goddess, Mahámáyá, who was passing by that place, and who had seen this action of Rámnáth, said, as a dreadful aerial voice, with great wrath and gnashing of teeth, "Villain, dost thou attempt to consume the body of the innocent Promodá, and thereby heap on thy head the crime of killing a woman? Dost thou not fear to commit this crime?" As Rámnáth went into a trance on hearing this dread voice, Srimanta and Promodá sat up, like persons on awaking. Finding Promodá revived, her formerly disconsolate husband was ready to die for very joy. "Life of life," exclaimed he, "the sight of your moon-like countenance has brought life into my dead body." He was thus giving vent to his feelings, when he saw Rámnáth insensible on the ground, at some distance. Taking him to be dead, he said with tears in his eyes, "Friend of my bosom! have you put an end to your existence, because I did not accept your word. If I happened to be guilty through ignorance, pray, do you forgive and answer me. Else I will make away with myself." Saying this, he took up a log of wood, and was going to strike it at his head, when Promodá snatched it away from him and cast it at a distance. Then Srimanta began to laugh, weep, dance, call Rámnáth aloud like a maniac. Seeing the plight of her husband, Promodá said, "O God! dost thou not relent, even after afflicting this wretch of a woman in innumerable ways? If it would be no better, it were far better for me to pass my days as a bird in this wilderness." She then took hold of Srimanta's hand and said in softly sweet accents, "Husband, if Rámnáth do not recover, it behoves us to resign our lives. But first let us offer up prayers to the Deity, for everything may be compassed through Divine grace. Let us bathe in this tank, and address ourselves to our devotions. If Rámnáth do not then receover, we will throw ourselves in this blazing pyre." Srimanta consented and said, "My mother has got me by worshipping Kátyáyaní. Let us worship even her. If my friend do not revive by this, we shall sacrifice ourselves in the pyre."

Then they made a clay image, and gathering wild flowers and blown lotuses, worshipped the goddess with them. Seeing all unavailing, they took rounds about the pyre, when, lo! a tottering old woman with a load of Sandal wood, supporting herself upon a staff, appeared before them, weeping loudly, and drawing near to Rámnáth, said, "I have left my home for a long time to go upon pilgrimages. I had my house here. Perhaps, it has been ruined for want of a protector. Where shall I shelter my head in this old age?" Then addressing Rámnáth, she said, "Who are you, fellow? Why do you obstruct my way by lying here? Have you no other place to lie down?" Saying this, as she struck the body of Rámnáth with her staff, lo! the young man sat up, and the old woman vanished. Having seen this marvel, Srimanta and Promodá said, "My Rámnáth, we were going to plunge into the pyre, taking you for lost, when an old woman, with loud wail, struck you with her staff. You have revived, and the old woman has vanished. Now, we should not tarry here a moment. We shall relate all, when we shall have removed ourselves to some other place." "For these days," replied Rámnáth, "we have not touched a morsel. Let me therefore procure some fruits from this forest. Remain here for some time." "Nay, you should not go alone," said his friend, "let us all go together." Promodá said "Let us first slake our thirst by drinking of this tank, and then think of going elsewhere, in search of food." Then thy descended to the tank, and slaked their thirst, by drinking water, each with his or her joined palms. After this, as they were going through the forest, they saw a beautiful building. Promodá said, "There's our residence."

Rámnáth was curious to enter in, but Srimanta objected to it, saying, "We have met with many misfortunes here. No need of seeing anything here." But his friend was importunate. So they entered the place, and went up to the first and second floors, and feasted their eyes with seeing the richly furnished apartments. They took it to be the residence of some god, for such odour was impossible in any human residence. They saw a quantity of various fruits in one chamber, as also savoury dishes of diverse kinds, the plates, in number three, and engraved each with a name, being of gold. At sight of these dishes, they looked around to see any human beings; but none was to be found. With apprehension, Srimanta said, "Without doubt, this place belongs to some god. We shall come to grief, if we tarry here." "Lord," said Promodá, "seeing this strange sight, my mind is swelling with thoughts, which I fear to tell you. If you believe, I will tell. Formerly, when we lived here, your wife Gándhiní used to prepare such dishes for us, daily. Probably, the day on which the anchoret cursed us, the girl had prepared these dishes for us, which have providentially remained in the same state. But this idea is wild, and you need place no faith in it. But the sight of the plates engraved with names convinces me of it." Then they examined them, and said, "All is possible to the Divine agency. However, we should make all haste to leave this place." Thereupon, as they were preparing to leave the house, an ærial voice said, "Ho! Where are you going, leaving ready food? If you reject this, you will fare ill." Hearing this superhuman speech suddenly, they knew not what to do,—when, lo! some person appeared before them, and said, "Friends, you need not fear: fall to." Then Srimanta said, "When repeated divine commands are heard, desiring us to eat, we should not hesitate." Then the three sat down to eat. When in the act of eating the wonderful dishes, it struck Srimanta that he had eaten such somewhere before. "Gándhiní used to cook so," said Promodá. Having finished, they washed their hands and faces, and chewed betels. They then came to the tank in the house, and were talking of departure, when they perceived a light in the sky, and were alarmed. The light neared, and now they could clearly see a stately fiery figure in a golden car. Seeing this, all trembled from fear. The fiery form alighted, and taking hold of all the three, took them into his car. Then he soared with his car to the sky. Srimanta spoke to the person in fear, "Sir, harm us not. We throw ourselves on your mercy." "No fear," answered the person. "All of you are dear to me. You needn't apprehend any danger from me." He then alighted at a golden palace, and entered in with his companions. The very touch of the ground filled Srimanta with delight; he thought that, perhaps, it was heaven itself; where else could such buildings be found? Then the blazing personage brought the three before the Gandarva, Puspa-danta, (flower-teeth), who was hearing music. Coming to him, he said, "My Lord, I have brought them from the Sandal forest; and they await your commands." Hearing this intelligence, the prince was excited, and said, "Where? Where is that youth? Hand him to me first." At this, Srimanta concluded that, it was no heaven, as he had falsely surmised; but Lanká, and that this man was its king. "He will eat me up, no doubt; otherwise, why should he be so eager to take hold of me, on hearing that we were come?" As the king extended his arms, the messengar handed Srimanta to him. The young man was terribly affrighted, and said with tears in his eyes, "O Lord of Rákshasas, pray do not devour me. I am the only son of my mother. I throw myself upon your mercy. I have not committed any wrong in your sight; save that we three had eaten the dishes that we found ready at the house in the Sandal forest. But that was not done by our own free will. The divine voice first enjoined us to eat, still we held out: the voice said a second time, 'If you neglect my word, you will fare ill.' We ate, in obedience to that behest. If we have erred in that, I beseech you to forgive us for our unconscious offence." The king of Gandarvas laughed at the piteous appeal of Srimanta, and said, "Why do you weep from fear? You have not transgrassed, neither is there any cause of fear. You think that I am a Rákshasa, and that I will eat you up. It is not so. My name is Puspadanta. I am your maternal grandfather. I have not seen you long, and it is for this reason, that I have brought you here. But do you first touch my eyes with your hand; then I shall tell you all." Then, as Srimanta touched the Gandarva's eyes with his hand, he received his sight, and eying the court around, and having rendered thanks to the Father of mercies, he took up the youth, and danced for joy. Then Srimanta, Rámnáth and Promodá paid their obeisance to the feet of the Prince and asked his grace. The court said, on the restoration of the prince's sight, "We consider ourselves blest at the removal of the curse, and the restoration of Your Highness' sight." Then the king took his three guests into the inner apartment. The queen could not contain her joy at the happy event; and said in tones thrilling with emotion, "Your Majesty, my happiness knows no bounds on your cure, and I can expect no higher joy than I feel at the sight of my grandchild. Now, may it please Your Majesty to point me out the child of my Sukeshá." "Does not Your Majesty remember?" said the king. "Our Sukesha is a human being now; her name is Tárávatí. This is her son, Srimanta. This girl, named Promodá is his wife, and this youth is the husband of Srimanta's sister." The king having explained this, they all three paid their reverence to the royal pair. The Queen stretched forth her arms, and embraced Srimanta. After pronouncing blessings on Promodá and Rámnáth, they enquired of the good news of Tárávatí. Srimánta informed his grandmother in detail of all the circumstances, and said to the king, "Your Majesty, I belong to the human race. I am quite ignorant of the manners and customs of the Gandharvas. I don't know which word gives offence, and which not. If you forgive me, I will ask Your Majesty some questions." The king was pleased with the humility of the young man, and said "Child, you are always at liberty to speak out your mind without reserve. Pray don't fear to do so. Whatever you may have to ask, I will answer." Then Srimanta asked, "O lord of Gandharvas! you say that my mother is your daughter. Then why did you curse her? Why again were you blind? I am extremely curious to know all this. May it please your Majesty to satisfy my curiosity in detail on all these points."

"My child," returned the king, "your mother was borne by my queen, and went by the name of Sukeshá. She daily paid her devotions to Kátyáyaní in the Vindya Mountains. Once, as she was going to worship, I called her on some business. She, however, went out without obeying me. This put me into a rage and I said, 'You have disbeyed my call. For this offence, you shall take a human form.' Then Sukeshá burst into tears and said, 'Father, it ill beseems a parent to punish his child more than is adequate. In virtue of your word, I shall have to be born among mortals. But do you confer this blessing on me, that the goddess Káṭyáyaní may be always propitious to me.' When Sukeshá thus prayed to me, I said, 'Be it so.' Then while I sat speechless in grief on account of my child, the ascetic, Garga, came in. On account of my absorption, I did not notice him. At this unconscious slight, the holy man flew into a rage, and exclaimed, 'O! hard-hearted Gandharva, you have cursed your unoffending daughter, and puffed up with the pride of wealth, has now slighted me, without deigning even to cast a glance at me! For this reason, you shall be struck blind.' At this terrible calamity, I rose up, and with fear and trembling threw myself down at the feet of the sage. At that time I could just see his feet. Afterwards losing sight of them, I took hold of the sage's feet and lamented loud. Seeing that I was disconsolate, the great man relented. He said, 'My word needs must take effect. But to console you, I will say this. When the daughter whom you have cursed will take her birth in the nether world, she shall bring forth a son, the touch of whose hand on your eyes will restore your divine sight.' Then in all humility I asked that best of sages 'O merciful sage! what personage will take his birth in the womb of my daughter; and how shall I come by him? Tell me this, holy sage.' 'You will learn every thing,' replied the anchorite 'if you worship the god of gods, Mahádeva, for a year, in the Kailásha mountains.' Saying this, the sage vanished. Then I began my austerities in the Kailásha mountains. At the end of a year, the god of gods, with Nadikeshwar, appeared before me, and said, 'O king of Gandharvas ! I am pleased with your prayers. Do you ask for a boon.' 'Lord !' said I, 'if thou hast been pleased with thy servant, then first restore his sight.' Mahádeva said, 'The word of a Rishi is infallible. You shall afterwards receive your sight, according to his promise.' Then I asked, 'God, by virtue of my curse, my daughter, Sukeshá, is now a human being. What great man will take his birth in her womb, the touch of whom is to cure my blindness ? And how will he, being a human being, come to the world of the Gandharvas ? Vouchsafe to tell this to thy devotee?' 'Lord of the Gandharvas,' replied the worshipper-loving God, 'Listen ! Once before this, in order to worship me, Kuvera brought flowers, garlands, Sandal-paste, and other articles necessary for worship, and went away to bring a quantity of Ganges water. In the meantime Ballika, the son of the Jaksha, Isu, came there strolling with his two wives. Seeing the fresh garlands, he took them up, and hung them on his own neck and those of his wives. On coming there, Nandikeshwar found that the articles of Kuvera had been desecrated ; and enraged at this, said, 'Impious wretches, as you have despoiled the articles set apart for worship, so you shall be born on earth.'

Then Ballika took hold of Nandikeshwara's feet, and wept. Nandikeswar said, 'You shall regain your native seat at the Gandharva heaven, after two births.' So the cursed souls were reduced to ashes. That Jakhya is now the son of a merchant in Uddípaní, named Chitrasena. His present name is Príyamvada, and his two wives were born in the family of another merchant, and have become his partners. The way in which Preyamvada, taking his birth in the womb of your daughter, will cure you of blindness, Nandikeshwar will reveal to you." Therefore, my child, through the grace of Nandikeshwar, I was kept informed of all that had befallen you. Then when you were cursed at Uddípaní, I gave you the supremacy of the Sandal forest and all that pertained thereto. All the things that you have seen there, belong to you. I have brought you here for my own sake."

All the circumstances that Srimanta had heard of from the ascetic, pertaining to the Sandal-wood, were detailed anew by the king of Gandharvas. Having heard all this, Srimanta began to hymn his grandfather. Being pleased with his humility and reverence, the king said, "My child, after so long, to-day has seen my troubles crowned with success. Now, whatever blessings you will ask at my hands, I will give you." Whatever blessings Srimanta asked were rendered him. Then he enquired, "Your Majesty, I was formerly the son of a Jakhya;—I am greatly curious to see my former parents. If you will, you can make me see them." In accordance with this request of his grandson, the king ordered a servant to call in the Jakha, Isu. The man immediately brought him in. On coming before the throne, Isu asked, "May it please Your Majesty to tell me why you have called me." Then pointing to Srimanta, the king said, "O Jaksha, do you recognise this gentleman?" "No, Your Majesty," replied the person, "I can't." Then the king of Gandharvas explained the relation between the two. Srimanta bowed down his head at the feet of his Jakhya father, and took the dust of his feet. The Jakhya took Srimanta in his lap, kissed and smelled his son's crown, and enquired for his good news. "My son, where are my two daughters-in-law now?" Srimanta hung down his head and answered, "Father, of my two wives, this lady is called Pramodá. She is my second wife; my first wife is at home." Then Pramodá worshipped the feet of her father-in-law, and related all the circumstances of her life. All rejoiced. Afterwards, Srimanta said to the king of the Gandharvas, in all humility, "I consider myself blest in seeing you, Sir. Now I am extremely anxious to see my mother. May it please Your Majesty to fulfil my wish." "Ho Jaksha," said His Majesty, "take Srimanta to your home, and satisfy him." Hearing this, the Jaksha said, "I will, Sire. I was only waiting for Your Majesty's command. Let me then take Srimanta with me." He thereupon took all three, and calling in his wife, said, "The son for whom you always weep, and who has gone to the nether world for the curse of Nandikeswar, is now before you." At this, the Jakshiní grew mad for joy, and seeing two men and a woman said, "Lord, which of the two is my Ballika ?" The Jaksha said, "This is your Ballika. He has received a human shape, and is called Srimanta. The other young man is Srimanta's brother-in-law. The lady you see is the younger wife of your son. The elder is at her house." When the Jaksha had given this information, they all three paid their reverence at the feet of the lady. She took Srimanta in her lap, kissed him and asked, "O son, how do you fare in your human form ?" Srimanta related every thing in detail. Then the Jakshiní said, "O son, do you once call me mother, and suck at my breast. I will confer this blessing on you. When you shall be hungry, on remembering me, your stomach shall be filled with mother's milk; and you shall get such an accession of strength that the most laborious work will not fatigue you. You shall be always victorious in war. You shall never grow old. Further I will give you a ring. In virtue of this, whatever you desire, you will have. In short, you will be equal to the gods in power. If anybody shall steal this ring, he will not be able to keep it; it will return to your finger. I will further tell you this. She in whose womb you have taken your birth, was formerly the daughter of a Gandharva. I used to worship Kátyáyaní with her in the Vindya mountains. For some cause she is now a mortal." Then Srimanta said with clasped hands, "Mother, tell me how you have obtained the ring you have favoured me with." "List, my child," said the dame. "In days of yore, at the churning of the Ocean, when rose Laksmí from the milky deep Ocean, presented the damsel to Nárâyana, and offered this ring to him as dower. Nárâyana gladly wore it on his finger. Afterwards, as he was worshipping the god of gods, with ten millions of lotuses, in order to test the reverence of his worshipper, Mahâdeva stole away a lotus. Knowing this, Nárâyana plucked out the eye that graced his forehead, and offered it to the feet of the god. The god was pleased, and gave him a lotus eye instead. Since then Hari goes by the name of the 'Lotus-eyed.' Nárâyana also offered this ring at the feet of Mahádeva. At this, the great god conferred the wished-for blessing and vanished. Then the lord of Umá gave this ring to his spouse. When Bhagabatí was preparing to go to her father, Dakha's ceremony, my father Kuvera decked out the damsel in jewels and gold, and among other ornaments, put this ring on her finger. My father gave it to me as my dower. Now I give it to you as a token of affection." Hearing this strange adventure of the ring, Srimanta was proud in possessing it; and said to his mother, with clasped hands, "Mother, I have a wish. If you permit, I will disclose it to you." "A son," replied the mother, "can demand anything of his mother. If the thing lie in my power, you shall have it, child." Then Srimanta said, "Mother, I am extremely anxious to see your father." "My child," returned the dame, "my father was angry with you. Therefore I cannot take you before him without knowing his mind. First, I shall acquaint him with your intention; then as he says, we shall do. Therefore stay here a little." She then went to Kuvera, and having gained his permission, brought Srimanta before him. Srimanta paid his reverence at the feet of his grandfather, and stood before him with clasped hands. Kuvera asked his daughter, "My child, is this your son, Ballika?" "Yes, Sire," returned the daughter. "He is my son." Then the king of Jakshas embraced Srimanta, and having enquired of his good news, said, "O child, I was in grief for your curse. To-day the sight of you makes up for all that. The blessings which have been showered upon you by the king of Gandharvas, and more especially the ring given to you by your mother, have well compensated your troubles; so that, although a mortal, you are equal to us in power." "Sire," replied the youth, "in your satisfaction is my best reward. Now I wish to wash off my sins, by seeing Nandikeshwar." Then the king of Jakshas appeared before Nandikeshwar with Srimanta, and after paying his reverence to the god, began to pray to him. Nandikeshwar was pleased with his devotee's prayer, and said, "Srimanta, you are blest. In your next life, you shall see Mahádeva." In the meantime, the ascetic, who formerly had appeared before Srimanta, came in with a smile. "What! Srimanta," said he, "do you know me?" Srimanta bowed at the feet of the sage, and said, "Sire, I have all my desires through your grace; nay, being a human being, I have seen heaven itself. What more can I expect?" Then the lord of Jakshas took farewell of Nandikeshwar, and returning to his own house with Srimanta, presented a loadstone to his grandson. "Your treasury," he said, "will always be full by the charm of this gem." In the meantime a messenger had come. He said, "Sirs, the king of Gandharvas is expecting your return. Pray, do not delay any more. Come there at once." Hearing this, the Jakshiní took her daughter-in-law in her lap, with tearful eyes, and blessed her, "My child, may you enjoy the perpetual spring of youth and be loved by your husband!" Then Srimanta, Rámnáth and Promodá bowed at the feet of the Jaksha couple, and asked their permission to go. The prince of Jakshas loaded them with presents, and they took their farewell. Then, on arriving at the house of the Gandharva king, Srimanta related all that had happened. The king said, "Srimanta, you have never seen a Gandharva court. To-day a court is to be held; come and see." Saying this, he took Srimanta and Rámnáth and came to the court. As they entered, the guests rose up, and welcomed them with every mark of respect. The king sat on his throne. Srimanta and Rámnáth sat on his left, on lower seats. The guests sat on their respective seats. Seeing the wonder of the company in seeing two human beings, the king, addressing the multitude, said, "Ethereal virtues! Of these two, this is my maternal grandchild. He was formerly a Jaksha, named Ballika. He has taken this form, by the curse of Nandikeshwar. He is no man. His touch has cured my blindness. It is to entertain him that we are assembled here." Hearing this, the guests were exceedingly glad. Then began music. Seeing and hearing things and sounds not seen by human eyes or heard by human ears, Srimanta and Rámnáth thought, "Is this divine enchantment or a glorious dream?" They wondered at it every moment. Then the meeting broke, and each wended to his own place.

The king of Gandharvas with Srimanta and Rámnáth, returned to his quarters, and they rested for the night. While asleep, Srimanta dreamed a dream, the purport of which was, that his mother Táràvatí, disconsolate for her son, was going into trances frequently. Seeing this, Srimanta cried from excess of grief. It awakened the people. They rushed in and saw that the youth was crying. The king of the Gandharvas took him into his lap, and with words of encouragement, asked, "Child, pray, why are you weeping?" Encouraged by the words of his grandfather, he told him of his dream. The king then said, "What fear for that? You shall go to your home this very night. Soothe yourself. I am going to make the arrangements." Pacifying him thus, the king went out.

On the other hand, Padmávatí was painting another dream on Táràvatí's mind. She dreamed that a

Brahminí, who had her husband, came to her and said, "Táràvatí, up! Your Srimanta is coming with his bride, accompanied with Rámnáth. Do you prepare the things necessary for receiving the pair auspiciously." Táràvatí started up in surprise, and related her dream to Dhanapati, whose joy knew no bounds. He immediately called his officers, and said, "Do you prepare the articles for worship, clean the temple, unfurl the flags, place pitchers with mangoe leaves, at intervals, and plantain trunks on each side." On receiving this order, the officers went about carrying it out. The women were engaged in procuring articles for auspicious rites. Then they, with the Brahmin ladies, remained gazing at the direction from which Srimanta was expected to come. The joy of Ketakí and Naliní was boundless;—every one knows the happiness that results from meeting with one we love. Ketakí said, "To-day we shall see the new bride." "Yes, my girl," said Naliní, "for a long time we have not seen our Prámodá." "Were you," replied Ketakí, "acquainted with her formerly; else how could you know her name to be Prámodá?" Naliní said with a smile, "I shall say nothing now; you will know all afterwards." From this, Ketakí could not know whether her companion's word was true or otherwise.

On the other hand, the king of the Gandharvas came to Srimanta and said, "All things are in readiness for your departure. Now, learn a bit of Gandharva lore." He then imparted some incantations to his grandchild. At this juncture, the Jakhya,

Isu, appeared with his wife, and affectionately taught his son many things. Then Srimanta bowed to the ground before the king of Gandharvas and that of Jakshas, and, after paying his reverence to his grandmother and mother, took farewell. The Gandharva king directed his retainers to conduct the three safely. Thereupon they told them to sit on a stone and close their eyes. "When we shall tell you to re-open your eyes, open them." When the three sat on the stone, the servants took the stone on their heads, and began their aërial journey. By order of the Jakaha king, fourteen jewelled barks stood ready in the king's harbour. The servants of the Gandharva placed the three on board one of the barks, and said, "Pray, re-open your eyes. You have arrived in your country." Then they did as they were asked, and saw that they were actually in their own country. At this they marvelled greatly. "How could we come here in a twinkling?" said Srimanta. "A little before this, we were on the heads of the servants. Wherefrom is this bark! We never came by the sea! How could all this befall?" Reading his thoughts, the men, with clasped hands, said, "All these jewelled barks have been presented to you by the Jaksha prince. They are yours." "This is true," said the servants of the Gandharva. "It is for this that we have placed you here." Hearing this, Srimanta thought, "Should the fame of all this wealth reach the ears of our king, he will surely not be able to resist the temptation. So let me call the king of Gandharvas." Upon this, he recited the

Gandharva incantations. "Appear, O king! appear eftsoons;—I burn to see you for the nonce."

Anon the Gandharva appeared and asked Srimanta, "Why have you remembered me in so short a time? Tell me. If you are in danger, I will arrest it in no time." Srimanta said, "Lord, the riches wherewith you have graciously enriched me are unattainable on earth. Our king may appropriate them by force. It is from this fear that I have called you." "Child," replied the Gandharva, "in virtue of your Gandharva lore, you can conquer the three worlds,—you know every illusion. I am always by you, on remembrance; so that there breathes not a soul in all the three worlds who can defeat or injure you. No fear. Now it behoves you to see all the riches that the Jaksha king and I have given you." Thereupon, the king showed him all the wealth, and related the virtues of every article. He then said, "It is about daybreak. See! see! the hare-spotted luminary is about to bid adieu; the sages are on their way to the river-side; the sun is advancing, swallowing the ocean of darkness, like Agastya of yore. The birds are leaving their nests, and with sweet notes are going in different directions." Saying this, the king vanished. When the day broke, the officers of the Gandharva fired guns. Hearing the reports, the keeper of the prince's harbour came, and enquired, "Wherefrom are you? Don't you know that nobody can come in without the permission of our prince? When you have dared fire guns and beat drums, you must be a hostile party. But see, yonder are fifteen ships furnished with guns. If you wish to live, fly away; else prepare to give battle. If you come for commerce, you should first obtain a letter patent from His Majesty, or else we shall not allow you to put your vessels in harbour. If you should belong to this country, let us know who you are, for your good." "Friends," replied Srimanta, "we are no foes, or foreign merchants. I am the son of the Srestí, Dhanapati. My name is Srimanta. I went for commerce. Now I have returned to my country. Do you convey intelligence of this to my father." On this the guards ran off to Dhanapati and reported the matter to him. Hearing this, Dhanapati, accompanied with his friends and priests, came to the shore. Seeing him, Srimanta and Rámnáth both alighted on shore, and paid their reverence to him. "O father," exclaimed Srimanta, "I am your worthless son. You have suffered greatly on my account. Do you forgive my transgressions?" Then Dayásindhu took Srimanta in his lap and consoled him with affectionate words. He then consoled Rámnáth, and seeing the many wonderful things that they had brought, said, "Far from seeing these things, my boy, I have not even heard their names." Some stood like statues at sight of the articles. Some said, "Srimanta is no common man, and why should not this be so? He who is blest by the goddess Mahámáyá can compass everything." All said,

"Let us all pray that Srimanta and Rámnáth may live long; and that they may revere Mahámáyá always. Then Dayásindhu placed her daughter-in-law in a litter, and went home.

Tárávatí, Ketakí and Naliní were expecting the entrance of Srimanta in the hall of Chandí, when Dayásindhu entered with his son, new daughter-in-law and son-in-law, and they all paid their reverence to the goddess. When Srimanta and Rámnáth bowed at the feet of Tárávatí, she, with tearful eyes, took her son in her lap, smelled his head, kissed him, and enquired for his good news. She then entered her house with her new daughter-in-law. All the citizens were loud in their praises of Táráví's fortune. Then she performed the *Stri-áchára* ceremony, as observed by her class. She then addressed her son, thus, "O son, I am blest with you. Pray do you eat a little now." When Srimanta had eaten, he sat by his mother and related his adventures. After listening him out, his mother said, "My Srimanta, how do I wish to see my father, the king of Gandharvas now! If you can make me see him, I then attain my desire." "Very well, mother," answered Srimanta, "you will see the prince tomorrow night." On the other hand, Ketakí was talking with her two sisters-in-law. Naliní said to Pramodá, "Sister, I cannot express my joy on seeing your moon-like face, after many a day." Then Pramodá laid the hanging end of her cloth around her neck, and bowing to the ground said, with tears, "Do you recognise me?" "Sister," replied Pramodá, "I am your servant for ever and a day. I have always thought on your feet. But owing to the malice of Fortune, you came by griefs for a time at my hands. Pray, excuse the past and smile on me." "The fortunes of both of us," rejoined Naliní, "are equal. How are you to blame? I have reaped but what Fortune had decreed. But tell me, tell me, how you have regained your husband." Then Pramodá began, "In virtue of the sage's curse, I lived a bird at the place, for the length of eighteen years. The day after that on which the curse had ended, our husband appeared at the place, and delivered me. The spot now goes by the name of the Sandal-forest, and is desolate now. But what is the wonder, the dishes you had prepared for us, had not been spoiled, but were fresh till that day. We fed on them. All this speaks of your greatness." She then narrated the incidents at the world of Gandharvas, and asked Naliní for a description of the way in which she had regained her husband. Naliní said, "Listen! When you had been changed into a bird, I appeared on the spot, and found our love a corpse. A person irradiating with fiery lustre, stood there. I took hold of the feet of the sage, and began to wail, when he related all that had befallen you two. He then said, 'Child, do not grieve more. You also are a virtuous girl. You shall regain your husband.' I then asked him, 'Lord, by what means shall I regain my lost lord?' Thereupon that best of ascetics said, 'With whatever desire you will resign your life at the junction of the Ganges with the ocean, shall be attained.' Accordingly I went to the place, and with the desire of regaining my husband, resigned my life; and having been born as the daughter of Vadra Sen, have regained our lord."

The girls were talking thus, when Srimanta entered and greeted them. They were thus engaged in sweet converse, when a maid-servant entered and said, "Sir, a messenger from the prince is at our place. The governor desires your presence." Hearing this, Srimanta went to Dhanapati, who said, "My son, the prince desires to see you; do you therefore go to the Presence with Rám. Present His Highness with whatever jewels you like." Having bowed at his father's feet, Srimanta took some precious jewels, and went to the king with Rámnáth. When they came to the gate, a warder went to the Presence, with this news. The king gave his permission for the entrance of the comers. The warder brought Srimanta and Rámnáth before the king. The king was on his throne, his unmarried daughter at his side; the officers were engaged in work. The king was struck with the beauty of Srimanta, and blessed God, for the delight at seeing a youth so transcendantly beautiful. "If he were of royal blood," thought he, "I would have married him to my lovely lily of a daughter." The courtiers were also affected; the daughter of the king gazed at Srimanta steadfastly. Seeing this, her maid-servant took her away into the inner apartment. Then when the king asked him to sit down, Srimanta sat and began to talk with the king. When Srimanta presented him the jewels, he thought, "Such gems are not to be found even in my treasury. I will ask him how he has come by these. Well, Srimanta," said he, addressing the youth, "tell me how you have come by such a priceless treasure?" Hearing this, Srimanta thought within himself, "Concealing the actual truth, I should tell the king that I have got them through superhuman agency." Thereupon he began, "May it please Your Highness, I went from Dravira to the Punjab for the purpose of commerce, and stayed there for three months. When I had acquired a sum of money there, I went to Ceylon. I prospered there, and at last embarked for home. On the fourth day of our voyage, the evening brought with it such a violent tempest, that the sailors were unable to save the ship. I was terribly frightened. Seeing no other means of saving my life, I tied together some gourds with a rope, and resigning myself to the mercy of Heaven, plunged into the boisterous deep. Your Majesty, the recollection of that day still fills me with fear. I can't say whether the ship weathered it or not. I went on floating, but could not say whither. The next day, about noon, I descried a sandy island. I went in that direction and reached land. But I could not walk from fatigue. For preserving myself, I fell on the ground on my knees. When I had dried in the sun, I looked around and found a child. 'How,' thought I, 'could this child come here. Perhaps, it has met with a like calamity with myself.' I came up to the child, and found that he was digging the ground and taking up heaps of gems. When I neared, he said with a smile, 'Do you once take me in your lap.' My lord, the sweet music of his lips made my heart glad. Anon, I took him up, when lo! all my bodily and mental uneasiness vanished. Then I asked him, 'Little thing! how came you to live here alone? Where are your parents?' He smiled and said, 'My parents are under these waters. I am digging up these gems for you. Do you take these away to your father and mother.' I again asked the boy, 'Do you once call your parents; I wish to see them.' 'My father,' said the child, 'lives sometimes in water, sometimes within the earth, at others in the air. See! See! My father is sailing through the air!' Saying this, he played with the dust, and taking out a fruit, gave it to me to eat. I gave half of it to the boy, who began to eat it with relish. I ate the other half, and it seemed to me as if I had eaten nectar. This world furnishes nothing like that sensation. Now the sun was sinking down to the west. The moon rose and spread his silver net.* At sight of this the boy was filled with glee, and began to play. When the noon of night had gone by, the boy told me, 'Look, your ships are coming.' I looked, and saw some ships. I took them to be some merchantmen, belonging to others. 'I am entirely at the mercy of God; if these men come in this direction, they will take pity upon me and take me into a ship.'

* The moon is a male in the Sanskrit literature.

I was thinking thus, when the boy said, 'What you are thinking is not the case. These are your own ships. At daybreak, you will go in and away to your home.' At morning, the ships landed. Now I saw that these were actually my ships. When the mariners saw me, they said, 'Sir, ever since you had leaped into the ocean, we had been searching you. Pray, get in.' Then when I asked farewell of the boy, he said, 'Do you fill your ships with the gems that I have collected.' In accordance with this, I ordered the sailors to do so, and they did it. Then when the boy entered the ship with me, the ships sailed. Both of us lay down on a bed, and when we felt inclined to sleep, the ships landed at your Majesty's harbour. The sailors sounded the *drum*, and we woke up. Seeing all these strange things, I was going to hymn the boy, when he said, 'Do you protect your fourteen ships. I go to my own place. Whenever any danger impend over you, I shall protect you.' Saying this, he vanished. As I was wailing his loss, the policemen of Your Majesty came to me and enquired of my name and lineage. Having furnished them with the information, I went home. Then as I was about to set out to see Your Majesty, in came Your Majesty's envoy. Father desired me to come to the Presence at once. I consider myself blest with the sight of Your Majesty. Having heard Srimanta out, the king eyed his minister askance, and said to Srimanta, 'Now you may go. We shall see you again at another time.'"

Seeing the delay of Srimanta in returning from the palace, both Naliní and Pramodá became anxious. On the other hand, when Srimanta had taken his departure, the king said to his minister, "The story of the merchant's son strikes me as untrue. He may have gained the gems from various countries; and from fear lest others should know of it, he has accounted for his acquisition by calling in the aid of supernatural events. However, my merchant is richer than those of other princes, every way." Then the minister said, with clasped hands, "Sire, I have not yet said anything from fear. Now I will deliver my mind." "Tell me," replied the king, "in detail." "Your Majesty," said the minister, "I am sure, the merchant's son is very cunning. He went to an island, as a trader, and having murdered the king, has appropriated all this wealth." "Nay, this doesn't stand to reason," replied the prince. "For had he done so, should none have heard of it? Would the king live alone? Would he not be attended by guards and chamberlains? Having regard to this immense wealth, the king should be possessed of great influence; and herein your opinion is falsified. But let me know your motive; whatever be the means whereby Srimanta has acquired this wealth!" "Sire," answered the minister, "All that Your Majesty says is true. But vouchsafe to lend your ear to what I say. Mansingha, Prince of Sindhu, was a powerful, famous, kind-hearted and merciful prince. He was always intent on increasing the happiness of his subjects. He did not even at intervals realise taxes from his people. For this, many became immensely rich in his dominions. There lived in his kingdom a man named Bhima Singha, who had acquired immense wealth, but who, notwithstanding, passed his days like a poor man. He had a son named Bejoy, who, from his childhood, had showed a superior intelligence and physical prowess. Once the boy went to his father and said, 'Father, to-day, I wish to see the prince; but I can't go without your permission.' Bhima Singha said, 'Why do you wish to see the prince, boy?' 'Without being known to the king,' replied the youth, 'a man has slender chance of increasing his wealth or fame.' 'Go, then,' said the father. Thinking that it was improper to go to the Presence, without presents, Bhima Singha prepared and gave him some. Then the youth said, 'Sire, pray give me some presents more; for if I do not please the minister first, he may speak evil of me to his master. But if I tie his tongue down by a golden chain, he will be a friend to me.' Hearing this, the father internally praised the good sense of his son, and adopted his suggestion. Accordingly he prepared other presents and sent his son with the things, with his servants and retainers. Bejoy arrived at the capital with his men, and after having secured his lodgings, and bathed and taken his meal, he saw the minister, and giving him the presents, expressed his wish to see His Majesty. 'To-morrow morning,' said the minister, pleased, 'I will take you to the court. I will introduce you to His Majesty; and if you have any suit, I will assist you in the matter.' 'Sir,' replied Bejoy, 'I depend entirely on you. Do you, Sir, make me acquainted with the prince.' He returned to his quarters, and having passed the night there, next day went to the Presence with the minister. After having bowed and offered the presents, he stood before the prince, when the minister began to give all the necessary information of the youth to the prince. 'May it please Your Majesty,' began the officer, 'Bhim Singha, a subject of Your Majesty, is very rich. This youth is his son. His name is Bejoy Singha. He is proficient in may branches of learning. Now he has come to pay his homage to Your Majesty.' Having been informed thus, the king examined the features and demeanour of Bejoy, and told him to sit. When he had sat, the king asked, 'Have you any suit? You may have your desire, if you express it.' Then, with clasped hands, Bejoy said, 'Sire, there are certain villages adjacent to the house of your servant. If it please Your Majesty to lease them to me, on condition of my paying a rent, Your Majesty will confer a boon on your servant.' 'You shall,' answered the prince, 'get the villages.' Then he told his minister to draw the lease, which being done, the minister had it signed by the king, and delivered it to Bejoy. Then Bejoy took farewell of the king, and having reached home, told everything to his parents, who were glad. Henceforth, Bejoy began to rule these villages, and paid the due annually. The clever Bejoy increased his wealth and attained influence over his subjects. Then he began to collect troops. When, in a short time, he had levied a force of twenty thousand men, Bejoy thought, 'Now I can obtain possession of the kingdom of Sindhu, for the king numbers only sixteen thousand troops; so that my force is superior to the royal army. Further, I am a strategist; so that in no respect is the king my equal. Should the king conclude peace, and give me half his kingdom, good and well; otherwise, I will beat him and take possession of the whole.' With this determination, he sent an ambassador to the prince. The man appeared before the prince, and after having paid his respects, began, as directed by his master, 'Bejoy Singha has sent me to Your Majesty. Sire, if you give half your territory to Bejoy Singha, and conclude peace, it will be well; else twenty thousand men, armed *cap-à-pie,* will fight against you desperately. Your Majesty may adopt the course you think best.' At intelligence of this, the king flamed with anger, and said, 'What! Being a jackal, Bejoy wishes to be a lion! For this, he shall have his reward ere long. Do you tell him to prepare for war. I will send him to hell, without delay.' When the messenger had left the place, the king ordered out his sixteen thousand, and marched.

On the other hand, Bejoy, hearing of the royal preparations from the envoy, stood ready with his army. Then the two belligerents met and began a dreadful conflict. When the fight had continued for a week, Bejoy Singha lost three thousand men; of the royal forces, some were wounded, some took to flight. Seeing the hopeless state of his fortunes, the ruler of Sinde, with his sword and buckler, began a single combat with Bejoy. Both fought skilfully; at length the king of Sinde became enfeebled. 'Your Majesty,' exclaimed Bejoy, 'you would not have been reduced to this pass, had you concluded a treaty then. Now it is for your good to render submission, unless you will lose your throne.' The king could return no reply from shame. 'Your Majesty,' again rejoined Bejoy Singha, 'I will show consideration by consenting to take one-half of your kingdom;—you may pass your days with the rest. But you must promise, that if any rebellion should break out in my dominions or should I be attacked by a foreign enemy, you would assist me. Conclude such a peace, and return to your capital.' The king concluded a peace to this effect, and returned to his home. From this, Sire, it is evident that it is extremely impolitic for a prince to allow any of his subjects to grow wealthy. I advise Your Majesty to secure the fourteen ships of the young man. Pray don't regard the merchant's son lightly. From his appearance and intelligence, I have entertained shrewd doubts." "Yes," replied the king; "I should try to secure all his wealth." "Your Majesty," replied the minister, "unless you imprison Srimanta, you can by no means secure the wealth in the ships. Should he come there, he will render material obstruction by his intelligence and wealth;—so that, if Your Majesty permit, we will imprison him." The king consenting, the minister sent a man to bring back Srimanta. The man came to Srimanta in hot haste, and said, "Sir, the minister calls you on some urgent business. Pray, come there instantly." At this, the young man thought, "I have just reached the end of the palace, after taking farewell of the king and minister; so that this call startles me. The minister must entertain some evil designs. But I have no fear, by the blessings of the Gandharva king." Thinking this, he went with the envoy. When Srimanta and Rámnáth entered the hall, the wicked minister, who was expecting them every moment, made a sign to the warder, who arrested the young man, and took them to prison. At this Srimanta laughed. Then the minister sent a message to the king, saying, "If Your Majesty permit, I will go myself and bring the jewels." Having obtained the king's permission, as the minister was going towards the ships, he thought, "I will first despatch all the most precious gems to my house. By this, I shall be more wealthy than the king."

On the other hand, Srimanta said to Rámnáth in prison, "The king's thoughts are evil; since he wishes to appropriate all my wealth, by imprisoning me. Now let me remember the king of Gandharvas." Srimanta remembered the Gandhárva Prince, who instantly appeared and asked, "Child! Why have you remembered me?" "Lord," answered Srimanta, "desiring to appropriate all the gems bestowed on me by Your Majesty, the king has imprisoned us, through the machinations of his wicked minister. It is for this reason that I have remembered you." "What is impossible to the gods," answered the king, "can never be possible to men. Now go home; I will adequately punish the king." According to the injunction of the Gandharva Prince, Srimanta and Rámnáth went home invisibly. The retainers of the Gandharva Prince (having received the necessary orders) immediately paralysed the hands and feet of the minister, and destroyed the motion of the guards; and they began to rain flesh and blood all round. They set up dreadful yells, and wearing frightful forms and dealing blows and slaps, disappeared like lightning. They caused instant stars to shoot in the city, and this frightened the people greatly. Seeing all these wonderful appearances, the king, trembling, called a council. He said, "All this is owing to my having imprisoned the merchant's son. Now if we release him, we can escape these dangers."

Deciding this, they went to the prison and saw that the minister lay senseless on the floor—he only retained his power of speech. On seeing the king, the minister burst out into tears and said, "Your Majesty, the son of Sádhu is no common man. For as soon as I had imprisoned the captives, they vanished, I know not where. My hands and feet are benumbed. Your Majesty, I have lost the power to get up. This is the fruit of my machinations." "Whatever it be," replied the king, "let us now ascertain the means of deliverance." They then concluded, "It is nothing else than divine agency;—we should therefore ask for forgiveness of our transgressions." They thereupon fell to praying to the gods. After a while, a divine voice said, "Thou hard-hearted villain—thou worst of monarchs! Thou imprisonedest the innocent son of Sádhu. It is for this sin that I have reduced thee to this plight. If thou canst install Srimanta as thy heir to the throne, and give him thy daughter in marriage, then only wilt thou find mercy; else thou art doomed." Hearing this, the king tremblingly said, "I bow to the divine behest; I will do as I am bid." As soon as the king had spoken thus, the servants of the Gandharva desisted from committing any further havoc. Then the king sat at court with his minister, and decided "to send an envoy to Dhanapati; and that should he decline, the king should go there in person."

On the other hand, the king of Gandharvas, having inflicted punishment on the king, appeared before Srimanta and said, "My child, I have punished your enemies. Now the king will give you his daughter in marriage and install you as his heir in the kingdom; for which an envoy is coming here. He will request you to go to the palace. If you decline to go, the king will himself come here. You should not therefore go with the envoy." "Lord," returned Srimanta, "I shall have my desire, if a palace be built with a forts at the extremity of the city." "Be it so," said the royal Gandharva, and calling Vishwakarmá, he issued orders for building the house, and then departed. The divine architect in a single night completed a palace with seven apartments, surrounded with a moat containing vessels upon the waters. The canal opened through sluices into the ocean, so that the supply of water would never fail. Valuable gems were set on the silver and golden walls, and the rooms were all the brighter for them. On the highways, he built brick houses, to serve for lighting the roads. When the palace had been built, Srimanta took the permission of the king of Gandharvas, and with his parents, friends and acquaintances, began to live in it.

On the other hand, the king having consulted with his ministers, wrote a letter and despatched with it a wise courtier to Dhanapati. The ambassador came to the gate of Dhanapati and sent the news by a warder. Dhanapati and Srimanta agreed to see the ambassador, and told the man to shew him in. The man went; and after having passed through the seven apartments, brought the envoy to Dhanapati. The envoy paid his respects to Dhanapati, who received him kindly. He then enquired for the good news of the king, and asked to know the occasion of the visit. The envoy thereupon handed the king's letter to Dhanapati, who read as follows:—

"I wish to bind my dearest child,
In wedlock with thy boy;—
My name to save, if thou dost come,
My mind will swim in joy.

Thro' force of Fate, I did thee wrong;
What's past is past for e'er;—
Thy suppliant I,—forgive me, pray,
And up my spirits cheer.

What pang was mine, when I thy boy
Kept fast in 'durance vile!'
Come here, Good Sir, with Srimanta,
To make my darling smile."

After reading the letter, Dhanapati remained silent;—at which the ambassador thought, "Perhaps, he has got angry with me and is silent." "I am infinitely obliged by His Majesty's letter," began Dhanapati, "since he has wished to give his daughter in marriage to my boy. But I can't believe it; for His Majesty can't do anything without the consent of his minister, since His Majesty imprisoned my innocent son by the advice of his minister. So that I think if we, father and son, go there, the king can easily take our lives. From this fear, I do not venture to go to the king, who is advised by so wicked a minister." Hearing the speech of Dhanapati, the royal envoy said with clasped hands, "Sir, whatever you have said is true. His Majesty imprisoned your son by the advice of the minister. For this he suffered great troubles; and prayed to the gods for deliverance. At last, a divine voice said, 'All this has befallen thee for having imprisoned the innocent son of Sádhu. If thou canst marry thy daughter to Srimanta, and install him thy heir, then only will thy troubles cease; else thy destruction is probably at hand. The minister has been put in chains for life.' Agreeing to this, His Majesty has sent me to you, gentle Sir. May it please you to go to the palace with your son, and thus save the empire. You may destroy the kingdom if you like, because your son, Srimanta, is no common man. He is a very god; he is ranging the earth in a human form." When the courtier had ended, Dhanapati said, "Do you remain here for to-day: to-morrow we shall do what we think best."

Here and there, there were various machines (instruments ?) in which were beautiful palaces of gold, shining with various gems. The king was unable to ascertain them fully,—he only understood that some rooms were made of lead and stone; some were made of white, red or blue marble. At intervals were crystal pillars. The gates, doors, &c., were made of ivory, silver or gold. The windows were decked with gems, and studded with pearls, corals, diamonds, rubies, moon-stones and sapphires. There were nine doors. Within the hall sat on a sapphire throne a red person; on both sides stood two others, —one white, the other red. One bore a sword; the other a buckler. From four springs fragrant waters flew upwards, and as they touched the ground, lo! they were changed into a chain of pearls. Anon issued two crystal damsels to take the chain; but they were demanded by the warders to desist. On this one fled; the other hung the chain on the neck of the personage on the throne, and went out. Then the chain melted. This process was then repeated.

In another room sat some monkeys. A cat was playing on an instrument—the mice were singing and dancing. At times, the monkeys with their black faces made various gesticulations, and showing their teeth in a laugh, fell down on the ground, and displayed many ludicrous expressions. Who could restrain his laughter at sight of this? Such a sight would dispel even deep grief. In another room, the air was dark with clouds, and it rumbled loud and deep; now and then the lightning flashed, and the thunder roared. Now, it seemed as if it were all daylight; anon it rained and hailed. In another room, a woman, who sat in the midst of flames, beckoned to all to come to her.

The king was seeing these wonderful sights, when a gate-keeper came to Dhanapati and informed him that the king with his courtiers was seeing the beauty of the palace. Hearing this, Dhanapati took Srimanta, and, seeing from a distance the pale countenance of the king, thought that nothing was impossible to the Divine agency. "He of whom thousands and thousands of kings are in fear, has come to my house without invitation. O God! thou canst do everything." Appearing before the Prince in this sad state of mind, father and son bowed at his feet; they craved his forgiveness for the past. After mutual embraces, Srimanta said, "Sire, I am the cause of your sorrow. But should you judge rightly, I am not to blame. First I had made known to you the supernatural events. But you did'nt believe me, through the evil advice of your minister." "No more of that, my child," replied the Prince. "Now, if you marry my daughter, Bhubana Mohiní, and consent to be installed as heir to the throne, then my dearest wish is attained." "Those feet which are unattainable by long prayer," said Dhanapati, "I have received easily. What more can I expect! Now, my prayer is, do you deign, Sire, to grace my house with your presence." Seeing the sincerity and kindness of Dayásindhu, the king thought, "I did'nt expect such kindness at the hands of those with whom I had behaved very cruelly. I should go to Srimanta's house." Dhanapati took the Prince to his house, and conducted him to a gemmed throne. The Prince sat upon it, and Dhanapati worshipped the royal feet. He then entertained the king sumptuously, and said humbly, "Sire, may it please Your Majesty to stay here to-day, and to go to the town to-morrow, early in the morning." At the sincere request of Dhanapati, the King consented, for his own interest. Táràvatí and other ladies began to see royalty through the windows. Dhanapati entertained his guests splendidly, and led the king to a milk-white bed. When it was late, the King rose and said, "What's the use of delaying more? Bring my Srimanta, and order my charioteer to get my car ready. I have determined to give my daughter to Srimanta to-day—no more delay." Dhanapati rose and went into the inner apartment. When he communicated the intelligence to Tárávatí, she said, "How can the marriage be celebrated to-day? More specially, as we have to ask the opinion of my father, the Gandharva king, and must act accordingly." Pleased at this advice, the merchant communicated it to his son, who said, "Then let His Majesty pass this night here. I shall request the Gandharva king to come over, and let me have his advice. We shall go together to the royal palace to-morrow morning." Agreeing to this, Dhanapati came to the king, and said, "Sire, I have no power to disobey the commands of Your Majesty; but may it please Your Majesty to comply with my request. I request you to pass the night here. I beseech you to do this." The king consented for his own interest. Srimanta went to Tárávatí and said, "Mother, to-day your father, the Gandharva king, will come here. If you wish to see him, pray get ready." When it was night, as Srimanta remembered the royal Gandharva, he appeared, and asked Srimanta, "Wherefore have you remembered me?" Srimanta answered, "Lord! may it please you to suffer yourself to be seen by my mother. Another word. According to your orders, the King has come here, and proposed the alliance. Now I await your decision." "Child," asked the king of Gaṇdharvas, "where is your mother? I will first see her, and then express my views."

Then as the King of Gandharvas was approaching Tárávati with Srimanta, she was suddenly struck with brightness as of the sun, and thought, "What's this? The sun never shines so in a room; more especially, as it is night." Reading the thought of Táráratí, the King of Gandharvas said, "My darling! I am your father, the King of Gandharvas. I have come to see you." And the lady, with tearful eyes, fell at the feet of her father, who took hold of her hands, raised her up, and wiped her face with his sheet. Srimanta led the king to a gemmed throne. Táråvatí stood at the feet of the Prince, and began to cast liquid glances on her father's face, and on the ground alternately. The royal Gandharva moistened his daughter with blissful tears. The ecstacy of joy at the happy union after so long a separation deprived both of speech—both remained mute for a while. Then the king said, "My love! No need of weeping more. I am always wishing for your weal. I have been unhappy ever since I cursed you. I had become blind, by virtue of a sage's curse, for having cursed you without reason. Your Srimanta has relieved me from blindness. Therefore I shall ever remember him." "Child," he went on, "you will never come by evil, by the grace of Kåtyåyaní." "Father," answered Tárávatí, in tones thrilling with emotion, "you are full of kindness. That you have deigned to show yourself to me has delighted me beyond measure. But the measure of my happiness will not be full so long as I do not see my mother. Father, how is my mother dear? Does she remember this forlorn wretch? Are my companions well? Is all well with the

Jaksha world? Father! father! how do I wish to see them!" "Child," said the Gandharva, "it is also the wish of your mother that you may soon go back to our house. But my wish is that your Srimanta may be monarch of this terraqueous world, and be the crown of kings, with his sons and grandsons enlightening the world with his fame and glory, and so making it more glorious than heaven itself. After this, when he will go to the Gandharva world, I will bequeath the empire to him, and go to the Himalaya to meditate on the God of gods. Therefore, my dear, do you enjoy earthly comforts for a length of time." After thus consoling Tárávatí, he gave his advice as regards the marriage of Srimanta with the king's daughter, and departed.

The next day Dhanapati came to the king of Magadha, and said, agreeably to the instructions of the Gandharva Prince, "Your Majesty, I have no objection to the match. But I am a merchant; Your Majesty is a Kshetriya. If you give your Kshetriya daughter to the son of a merchant, the other princes may prove hostile to you, and bring disgrace upon your hitherto unblemished line. Your Majesty should therefore act with the consent of the Kshetriyas. Your Majesty should go to your capital and invite all the subordinate Princes. When they shall have arrived, I will come to you with Srimanta."

The king consented to the advice of Dhanapati, and on the eve of leaving the place said, "What you have said is good. But should the princes object to the match, and take up arms, how should I defeat them?" "Your Majesty," replied Dhanapati, "need not fear on that score. Bless my Srimanta. He alone will do everything." Thereupon the king went to his house. On reaching home, he sent invitation letters to the kings of Anga, Banga, Kalinga, Tailanga, Sauráshtra, Drávira, Magadha, Andra, Kásí, Kánchí and Abantí.

Durjoy Singha, king of Andra, got wroth in receiving the letter, and said to his counsellors, "Ho! Sirs! what do you think is here? The prince of Magadha is going to give his daughter in marriage to the son of a merchant. What do you advise?" Then the counsellors said with clasped hands, "Sire, Your Majesty is a king. You can do anything you like. It would be better on the part of Your Majesty to consult other princes as to the propriety of going there or not." "We should expel the king of Magadha," said the prince, "and taking his daughter by force, bestow her on a Kshetriya; else the Kshetriyas will come to disgrace by this *mésalliance*. Do you therefore make known my mind to all the other princes, that they may at once come with their armies." Agreeably to this injunction, the minister wrote to the princes. They soon came with their forces, and meeting with Durjoy Singha, marched to Magadha. Having encamped there, they sent an ambassador to the king of Magadha. The messenger came to the prince and said, "May it please Your Majesty! Durjoy Singha has come here with the princes of various countries. If Your Majesty wishes to save your country, you should pay tribute to Durjoy Singha, and give him your daughter; else the fight would take place to-morrow, early in the morning." The king of Magadha was frightened, and calling in Srimanta, acquainted him with the message. Srimanta said to the messenger, "Tell your king to prepare for battle to-morrow, early in the morning." Having done this, he went to his own house, and remembered the servants of the Gandharva king, who immediately appeared. "Of those who will come to fight to-morrow," said Srimanta, "do you benumb the hands and feet of all, excepting the kings." Then he called the general of Magadha and said, "To-morrow do you lead your forces to the field, and be present there." The general accordingly spread a proclamation in the army regarding the coming fight. The men, amounting to sixty thousand, well equipped, appeared on the field before daybreak. Then Durjoy Singha came to the field with the princes, surrounded by the forces. First the word-fight, then the arms-fight—there was great uproar. Then Srimanta entered the field on horseback, and saw that the Magadha forces were being beaten. He remembered the Gandharvas, who came invisibly and sent such shouts that the hostile forces fainted on hearing them. At this opportunity, the Gandharvas fell to benumbing their hands and feet, and depriving them of their weapons. After a while they recovered, but had no motion. The kings saw the condition of the troops, and despaired; when the Gandharvas chained Durjoy Singha, the king of Udra, and having conveyed him through the air, imprisoned him in the jail of Udra, and liberated the prisoners. Seeing these wonderful things, and the pitiable condition of the king, the guards hastened to the minister, who came to the prison with the king's son. They wept on seeing the king. Then they called a blacksmith, whose hands became themselves fast shackled as soon as he tried to cut off the king's chains. As many persons as tried to cut the chains became enchained themselves. The rumour spread that all the inhabitants were being imprisoned; so that thinking it expedient to leave the country, the inhabitants began to desert it. Seeing this, the minister thought that it was nothing else than the might of Srimanta. "So that unless I go to that great man with the king's son, there is no hope of saving His Majesty." Learning this, Durjoy Singha advised his son to go to Srimanta with the minister. On the other side, witnessing the deplorable plight of the troops, the assembled kings began to ask Srimanta to have mercy, and agreed to pay tribute to him. Srimanta said with a smile, "You needn't be apprehensive; the armies will be restored to their natural condition. Pray, do you dismiss your troops, and remain here some time." As soon as he had said this, the host was restored to its natural condition. The kings sent their respective armies to their countries, and remained behind. When the banner of Srimanta's victory floated in the air, the king of Magadha said to his minister, "To-day will take place the nuptials of Srimanta and my daughter; so do you prepare for the ceremony, and making ready for the assembly, bring Srimanta and Dhanapati. Invite also all the princes to the assembly." Having received the orders of His Majesty, the officers prepared everything. In the evening, Dhanapati arrived at the court with Srimanta. When the princes were assembled, the king of Magadha gave his daughter, Bhubanamohiní, to Srimanta, according to all the sanctimonious rites. Srimanta entered the bridal chamber with the princess. The king entertained Dhanapati in a richly furnished apartment. He entertained the princes with banquets; and then they retired to their appointed quarters.

Next day, on Srimanta expressing his desire to go home, the king called the priests and courtiers, and at an auspicious hour invested Srimanta with the insignia of royalty.

Then, when the princes had met to pay tribute to the new king, Cheit Sing, son of Durjoy Singha, came before Srimanta with his father's minister, and said with clasped hands, "Sire, save Durjoy Singha, our king." "I am a merchant," said Srimanta; "Durjoy Singha is a Kshetrya—a puissant prince. How can I save him? If you can in all humility crave the forgiveness of the king of Magadha before all the princes, then only can you find relief. Else there is no hope." Cheit Sing said, "Whoever touches my father is involved in his fate! How then can we bring him here?" Saying this, he fell down at the feet of Srimanta, and began to cry. Srimanta was naturally kind-hearted; he was touched with the grief of Cheit Sing, and said, "Do you stay a little. Your father will be here presently." Then Srimanta called the servants of the Gandharva, and said, "Do you bring Durjoy Singha through the air, and place him at the feet of His Majesty of Magadha." They brought Durjoy Singha in a short time, and placed him at the feet of the king of Magadha. The kings were awe-struck with the sight of this, and fell to praying. Srimanta told them to be of good cheer, and said," "Your Majesty, this person is called Durjoy Singha. It is he who was the head of all these princes. He is very proud. If he has offended you through error, pray forgive him. If you permit, I will release him." "The great should regard the honor of honorable men," answered the king. Then at a signal from Srimanta, Durjoy Singha was released by the Gandharvas, and he thereupon began to pray. Then the king of Magadha embraced Durjoy Singha, and made him sit by him. "Princes," said he, "I have given my daughter to Srimanta, and have invested him with the offices of royalty; you should pay him tribute; I retire from this government." Hearing this, the kings paid Srimanta tribute. The heavens now rained blossoms. Then, when the princes asked farewell of king Srimanta, he said,

"You have suffered no end of troubles at my hands. Do you therefore deign to come to my house and dine." The princes consented. The young king then took farewell of his royal father-in-law, and went to the inner apartment. The ladies decked out Bhubanamohiní, and performed the *siri-áchára* ceremony. Srimanta thought, "Since I shall have to go home with the princes, I should have a divine car." Having decided thus, he expressed his intention to the servants of the Gandharva. They fetched a divine car. Having ascended the wonderful car, as the astonished princes were extolling Srimanta, Durjoy Singha thought, "Where else shall I get such a good bridegroom? Therefore I will also give my daughter to Srimanta." He then with clasped hands expressed his desire to Srimanta. The latter said, "Sir, I will let you know my mind to-morrow." Having beguiled the way by such talk, they arrived at Srimanta's house.

The inmates took the bride into the inner apartment. Rámnáth appointed servants to wait on the princes. There were no bounds to the joy of Tárávatí. Naliní and Promodá* made merry with the princess. The princes dined. They admired the wealth of Srimanta, and extolled his 'mighty magic.' When it had got late, Srimanta remembered the Gandharva king, and said, "Sir, I wish to show the Gandharva court to these assembled princes. But how can I do so without your permission?"

* Her other name is *Promodiní.*

"What's the wonder?" answered the Gandharva. He thereupon called his servant and said, "Do you bring my theatre and court from the Gandharva world to the house of Srimanta within three hours, and invite the Jakhas and Gandharvas. Bring the dancing girls of heaven to sing and dance. Never disobey any orders which Srimanta may issue." Having given these directions, the Gandharva went to his own place. Then the servants brought down the Gandharva court. The Jakhas and Gandharvas came. The Kinnaris began to sing and dance. It is not possible for any human pen to describe the beauties of the court; for having heard of it, Indra himself came and sojourned there. Then when the servants informed Srimanta of the establishment of the Gandharva court, Srimanta sent a heavenly car to Kisarilál Singha for his conveyance. The king arrived at Srimanta's place and learnt all. Then Srimanta informed the princes who came before him. He said, "I have prepared a court for the entertainment of Your Highnesses. Pray, deign to grace it with your presence. I have also got some royal robes, by supernatural means; I shall feel obliged by your accepting them." Saying this, he made a signal to the servants, who immediately fetched some robes, glittering with gems. The princes took them, and considered themselves as above human nature.

The king of Magadha came with Dhanapati, and surveyed the splendour of the court. The kings thought, "Have we come to Heaven! Have the ethereal substances of the gods become visible to mortal sight! What a wonder! But how can we enter into the fiery splendour?" Knowing their surprise, Srimanta said, "This is no fire; this is the lustre of the court, and the flaming glory of the Gandharvas and Jakhas. You need not be apprehensive. Pray, enter the court without fear."

When Srimanta entered the court with the princes, the king of Magadha and Dhanapati were led to the higher seats. Srimanta sat by them on a lower seat. The princes sat on their respective seats. Now the Apsaras began to sing and dance. Their music charms the gods themselves—not to say of men. Indra saw the assembly from the sky, and rained blossoms. All the guests, excepting Dhanapati, Srimanta and the princes, had eyes which had no twinkling, and bodies without their shadows. They had never before touched the earth. Seeing all these supernatural things, the kings thought themselves blest. The court broke with the dawn; and each wended to his own place.

The next day Srimanta called the king of Andra and said, "To Your Highness' proposal of yesterday, I have no objection. But I won't marry again. If you wish to enter into relationship with myself, do you then give your daughter to my first wife's brother, Kirti Chandra Roy. He is no common man; he is the son of the noble Vadra Sen Roy of Rámnagar. He is in my house. If you permit, I will call him." Then Srimanta ordered a servant to call Kirti

Chandra to the court. Durjoy Singha saw the young man, and said to Srimanta, " If I have to give my daughter to any other than Your Majesty, I will give her to him." The match was settled, and the minister was sent to bring the damsel. At an auspicious hour, Durjoy Singha gave his daughter to Kirti Chandra. Then Srimanta bade farewell to the princes, appointed Rámnáth as his minister, and began to reign happily.

During the reign of Srimanta, the earth yielded abundant harvests, the kine were filled with nectar, the highways were safe, and the subjects were virtuous. After some time, both wives of Srimanta were in the family way. When it was full ten months, they gave birth to two sons, bearing all the auspicious marks. The palace overflowed with joy. The delight of Dhanapati and his consort on seeing their grand-children may well be conceived. Then the *annaprásana* and other ceremonies were celebrated. The boys grew up like the moon and increased the happiness of their parents. When they reached the age of five, they were placed under the tuition of a good teacher. Afterwards the two wives of Srimanta brought forth two daughters. Rámnáth had a son. The sons of Srimanta in a short time became versed in the arts and sciences. When the sons and daughters became marriageable, Srimanta married them. After enjoying the throne, he made over the sceptre to his eldest son, Vírbáhu. Then Tárávátí began to pray :—

"O Bhagabati, thou hast been pleased to confer royalty on my Srimanta. May thy kindness always last!"

In the meantime a messenger had come from the Gandharva world and said, "Your Majesty, the king of Gandharvas has expressed his intention of going to the Himalayas for devotion. He has therefore desired you to go to him, with your friends and relatives; so that he may make over to you the charge of the kingdom." Srimanta dismissed the emissary by intimating that he should meet with the Gandharva prince in a fortnight. He then consulted with his parents and the ex-king of Magadha, and called the dependant princes. "Your Highnesses," said Srimanta, "I shall now go to the Gandharva world, with my friends and relatives, to rule there. If you render the same homage to my son, that you have done to me, I hope you will reign in peace." He then imparted the Gandharva incantations to Rámnáth and said, "Do you now remain here for sometime. Whenever necessary, you will be able to go to the Gandharva world, by virtue of the incantations." Next he called his two sons, embraced them and smelled their crowns. "You will reign in perfect happiness," said he. "Show your affection for His Highness, Durjoy Singha. You must also regard the honor of these princes." He was speaking thus, when a glorious car descended from heaven, when Srimanta said, "Farewell to all! If I have been guilty of any offence, pray excuse me." At this, all began to weep.

Then Srimanta entered the car with Dhanapati, Tárávatí, the ex-king of Magadha and his consort, and Srimanta's two wives; and began to go through the air. Seeing this wonderful sight, all stood like statues. In a short time the car disappeared, when the spectators felt sad. They then began to go to their quarters, praising the glory and might of Srimanta.

END.

THE

TWENTY-TWO MUSICAL SRUTIS

OF THE

HINDUS:

BY

RAJAH SIR SOURINDRO MOHUN TAGORE.
BAHADOOR, Mus. Doc.,

Knight of the United Kingdom of Great-Britain and Ireland; Companion of the Order of the Indian Empire; Grand Cross, Grand Officer, Commander, or Knight of divers Orders of Chivalry; Officer of Public Instruction, France:

Nawab Sháhzádá of the Persian Empire, Sangitá-Náyaka; &c., &c.

Calcutta:

PRINTED BY I. C. BOSE & CO., STANHOPE PRESS, 249, BOW-BAZAR STREET, AND PUBLISHED BY THE BENGAL ACADEMY OF MUSIC, PATHURIAGHATA RAJBATI.

1886.

The Srutis with reference to their position in the Octave.

Names of the Seven Notes.	*Names of the Twenty-Srutis.*
C—SHARJA (Tonic)	Tívrá 1.
	Kumudvatí 2.
	Mandá 3.
	Chhandovatí
D—RISHABHA (Super Tonic)	Dayávatí 5.
	Ranjaní 6.
	Ratiká 7.
E—GÁNDHÁRA (Mediant)	Raudrí 8.
	Krodhá 9.
F—MADHYAMA (Sub-Dominant)	Bajriká 10.
	Prasáriní 11.
	Príti 12.
	Márjaní 13
G—PANCHAMA (Dominant)	Kshiti 14.
	Raktá 15.
	Sandípaní 16.
	A'lápiní 17.
A—DHAIVATA (Super Dominant)	Madantí 18.
	Rohiní 19.
	Ramyá 20.
B—NISHÁDA (Leading Note)	Ugrá 21.
	Kshobhiní 22.
C—SHARJA (Tonic) (*Higher.*)	Tívrá. (*Higher.*)

TO

His Excellency the Right Hon'ble

THE EARL OF DUFFERIN,

K. P., G. C. B., G. C. M. G., G. M. S. I.,

&c., &c., &c.,

Viceroy and Governor-General of India,

THIS PAMPHLET

IS

MOST RESPECTFULLY DEDICATED

BY

HIS EXCELLENCY'S

MOST OBLIGED AND HUMBLE SERVANT,

S. M. TAGORE.

THE

TWENTY-TWO MUSICAL SRUTIS

OF THE

HINDUS.

THE classical authorities on Hindu Music thus describe the phenomena of sound :—

When the animal soul wants to speak out, it impresses the mind into its service, and the mind acts on the fire that has its seat in the abdomen. Thus moved, the fire mixes itself with the vital air that pervades the ligament known as *Brahma Granthi* which lies below the navel. The vital air gets inflated in consequence of contact with the fire, and gradually rises up, causing, in the navel, the *Ati Sukshma Náda* (or the very minute sound,) in the chest, the *Sukshma* (or the minute,) in the throat, the *Pushta* (or the developed,) in the head, the *Apushta* (the suppressed,) and in the mouth, the *Kitrima* (or the artificial sound). The theory described as above is best illustrated by the meaning of the term *Náda* which is composed of the two consonants *Na* and *da*, the former signifying the vital air, and the latter, the fire.

The following description of the production of sound is taken from Nathan's well-known work "Musurgia Vocalis"—"An Essay on the History and Theory of Music, and of the qualities, capabilities and management of the human voice:"—

"Sound is produced by the reverberation of air. When any elastic body is caused to vibrate, it acts upon the circumambient fluid of air, and creates in it pulses, waves, or undulations, which again acting or striking upon the *tympanum* or drum of the ear, communicates with ur senses and gives to us the idea called *sound.*"

"The varieties of tones in human voices," continues Nathan, "arise partly from the dimensions of the *trachea* or wind-pipe, which, like the flute, the longer and narrower it is, the more acute is the sound it gives, but principally from the head of the *larynx* or knot of the throat, called *pomum adami*, the tone of the voice being more or less grave as the *rima* or clef therein is more or less open. Hence, according to the different qualities of musical *sounds*, we have *a thin tone,—a full tone,—a harsh tone,—a rough tone,—a round tone,—a rich tone,—a liquid tone,—a mellow tone, &c.*"

Again :—

"The office of respiration, or breathing, comprehends two processes, namely inspiration, by which the common air of the atmosphere is drawn inwards so as to inflate the lungs; and expiration, by which it is discharged so as to collapse the air-cells, and thereby diminish the capacity of the lungs in proportion as it was increased by the former function. And although these processes are continually going on with great rapidity in the living system, it is still in our power to repress or protract either of them at pleasure to a considerable extent, and thereby to render them subservient to the rules of music. The *trachea*, or wind-pipe, with its several appendages, is of vast importance in the management of the voice, which is considerably governed by its contraction and elongation; but more particularly by that of the *larynx*, a cartilaginous body, which may be considered the commencement of the *trachea* and its common reservoir of air. It is composed of five annular cartilages placed above one another, and united by elastic ligaments, or fibres, by which it is dilated and contracted, so as to be capable of producing all the various tones of voice. It is distinctly seen rising in the production of acute tones, and descending in low ones. For the purpose, therefore, of effecting the greatest possible elevation of this organ, we almost involuntarily throw back the head in great efforts of singing.

"'The *larynx,*' observes Rennie, 'is lined internally with a very sensible, vascular and mucous membrane; which is a continuation of the membrane of the mouth. It is of great importance to keep this in view, as it is owing to its becoming irritated or inflamed and throwing out a quantity of tough phlegm, that hoarseness arises, and other disorders of the voice.'

"At the top of the *larynx*, we have two semi-circular membranes forming a small oblong aperture, the opening of the wind-pipe, which can be dilated or contracted at pleasure and by its vibratory motions, the tones of the voice are modified; this is termed in anatomy the *glottis*."

To resume the description according to the Sanskrit authorities. The sound produced in the chest is termed *Mandra*, that in the throat is called *Madhya*, and that in the head, is styled *Tára*. On this subject Nathan has the following :—

"The qualities of the human voice are commonly distinguished under three heads, according to the natural organs which appear most particularly concerned in its modulation and tones :—1*st*, where the sound appears to issue almost entirely from the lungs, it is distinguished as a *chest voice*, called by the Italians, *voce* *di petto* ; also, *voce naturale*, the natural voice : 2*ndly*, where the throat appears the organ connected with the production of sound, it is called a *throat voice*, termed in Italian, *falsetto* : 3*rdly*, where the process of breathing seems more than usually connected with the nostrils, and the sound is accordingly modulated by their influence, it is termed a *head voice*, in Italian, *voce di testa*."

Each of the kind of sound defined as *Mandra*, *Madhya*, and *Tára*, is divided into twenty-two parts, each of which comes under the designation of *Sruti*, so called because it is perceptible to the organ of hearing.

The classical authorities are divided in their views on the subject of *Srutis.* According to some, *Srutis* are of two kinds—*viz, Svaragata,* or those which are inherent in the seven principal notes, and *Antara,* or those which intervene such notes. Those that support the seven principal notes come under the designation of *Svaragata,* and those that represent the intervals between the seven principal notes are classed as *Antara.* According to others, *Srutis* are of three classes in accordance with the three different seats of sound. Some others, again, affirm that *Srutis* are twenty-two in number, and designate them as follow:—

(1) Tívrá; (2) Kumudvatí; (3) Mandá; (4) Chhandovatí; (5) Dayávatí; (6) Ranjaní; (7) Ratiká; (8) Raudrí; (9) Krodhá; (10) Bajriká; (11) Prasárini; (12) Príti; (13) Márjaní; (14) Kshiti; (15) Raktá; (16) Sandípaní; (17) A'lápiní; (18) Madantí; (19) Rohiní; (20) Ramyá; (21) Ugrá; and (22) Kshobhiní.

Those who fix the number of *Srutis* at sixty-six, (at the rate of twenty-two to each of the three seats of sound,) name them as under:—

I.—For the Seven Notes in the *Mandra* octave.

(1) Mandrá; (2) Atimandrá; (3) Ghorá; (4) Atighorá; (5) Mandalá; (6) Saumyá; (7) Sumaná; (8) Pushkará; (9) S'ankhiní; (10) Nílá; (11) Utpalá; (12) Anunásiká; (13) Ghoshavatí; (14) Nílanádá; (15) A'vartaní; (16) Raṇadá; (17) Ekagambhírá; (18) Dirghataṛá; (19) Nádiní; (20) Mandrajá; (21) Suprasanná; and (22) Ninadá.

II.—For the Seven Notes in the *Madhya* octave.

(1) Nádántá; (2) Nishkalá; (3) Gurhá; (4) Sakalá; (5) Madhurá; (6) Galí; (7) Ekákshará; (8) Bhriñgajáti; (9) Rasagíti; (10) Suranjiká; (11) Púrṇá; (12) Alankáriṇí; (13) Báñs'iká; (14) Baiṇiká; (15) Tristháná; (16) Susvará; (17) Saumyá; (18) Bháshâñgí; (19) Várttiká; (20) Sampúrṇá; (21) Prasanná; and (22) Sarvabyápiniká.

III.—For the Seven Notes in the *Tára* octave.

(1) I's'varí; (2) Kaumárí; (3) Savarálí; (4) Bhogavíryyá;

(5) Manoramá; (6) Susnigdhá; (7) Divyáñgá; (8) Sulalitá; (9) Vidrumá; (10) Mahárká; (11) Sañginí; (12) Ráká; (13) Lajjá; (14) Kálí; (15) Suskmatisukshmá; (16) Pushtá; (17) Supushtiká; (18) Vispashtá; (19) Rokarí; (20) Karálí; (21) Visphotántá; and (22) Mediní.

We do not agree with those who, as we have shown above, fix the number of the *Srutis* at sixty-six. As the fact of there being three places in the human body (from which proceed the sounds representing the three octaves) does not make the number of the principal notes twenty-one instead of seven, it does not stand to reason that the *Srutis* which form the intervals of the octaves would have to be multiplied by three to represent the three octaves. In fact the *Srutis* have lower or higher values according as they represent the intervals of the lower or higher octaves, precisely as the notes in the octaves have, according to the positions of the octaves.*

* Perhaps, the object which the authorities had in assigning a name to each interval in the three octaves is to afford one facilities to trace the position of a particular *Sruti* by the bare mention of its designation.

It would, perhaps, be more reasonable to accept the theory of those who declare the number of *Srutis* to be countless; for there is an authoritative text to the effect that "even *Brahmá* found himself unable to enumerate the *Srutis* intervening the musical notes." We, however, are decidedly of opinion that the number of *Srutis* is twenty-two, and proceed to delineate them accordingly.

For the purpose of causing an idea of the nature of the *Sruti* to be formed, the scholars of old have said this much only :—Above the chest lies the tubular vessel called *Sushumná-nárí,** round which are arranged in a crooked way twenty-two very minute arteries. The vital air, referred to in the preceding pages, comes into contact with these, in the course of its motion upwards, and produces each of the twenty-two *Srutis.* These *Srutis* rise in value—each higher than the preceding one. Thinking it hard to impress upon one the idea of the *Sruti* by means of the voice, the classical scholars have laid down the following

* One of the three canals, which, according to the anatomy of the Schools of Indian philosophy and medicine, are the chief passages of breath and air.

directions with the object of illustrating their views on the subject :—

Mount a *Víṉá* (a stringed instrument) with twenty-two strings. Tune the first string so low that if it is tuned lower the sound would be perfectly inaudible. Tune the second, a *little* higher than the first, but so as not to admit of the production of any perceptible sound between the first and the second; and so on, as regards the other strings. The sound produced by each of the strings thus tuned will represent a *Sruti*, and the consecutive sounds will represent the sounds emanating from the twenty-two *Srutis*.

We, however, have hit upon another method to ascertain the nature and the position of the *Srutis*. The method is as follows :—

Take a *Setár* or a *Víṉá*; measure the distance between the *Sharja* (C) of the *Madhya* (middle) octave and the *Sharja* of the next higher octave, *i. e.*, the C of the *Tára* octave. Divide the space between these two *C's* by putting a dot or a line in the middle. Put a dot or line on either extremity. Place the note F over the dot or line in the middle, the note C on the other extremity of the first-half portion of the divided space, and the note higher C on that of the second-half portion. Sub-divide the first-half portion into nine equal and the second-half into thirteen equal parts, and put a dot or line to mark off each sub-division. Including the dots or lines already put in (which respectively represent C and F), and excluding the one which represents the higher C, there will be in all twenty-two dots or lines. Now, each of these dots or lines will represent a *Sruti* and the total number of *Srutis* will necessarily be twenty-two; the names of which have already been given in consecutive order. Of these twenty-two *Srutis* are born the seven principal notes,–*Sharja* (C); *Rishabha* (D); *Gándhára* (E); *Madhyama* (F); *Panchama* (G); *Dhaivata* (A); and *Nisháda* (B).

The place indicated by the position of the first *Sruti* (*Tívrá*) represents *Sharja* (C).

The place indicated by the position of the fifth *Sruti* (*Dayávatí*) represents *Rishabha* (D).

The place indicated by the position of the eighth *Sruti* (*Raudri*) represents *Gándhára* (E).

The place indicated by the position of the tenth *Sruti* (*Bajriká*) represents *Madhyama* (F).

The place indicated by the position of the fourteenth *Sruti* (*Kshiti*) represents *Panchama* (G).

The place indicated by the position of the eighteenth *Sruti* (*Madantí*) represents *Dhaivata* (A).

The place indicated by the position of the twenty-first *Sruti* (*Ugrá*) represents *Nishháda* (B).

The annexed Table explains the position of the *Srutis* with reference to the Diapason.

Great difference of opinion

exists as to the relation of the *Srutis* to the notes. Some think that they being both perceivable by the ear are one and the same in nature. But this opinion does not appear to be a sound one, for the *Sruti* is the foundation or supporter of the note, and consequently the supported cannot be the same as the supporter. Others hold that the note is reflected on the *Sruti* just as the human face is reflected on the looking-glass. This view, too, does not seem to be above refutation, for, unlike that of the note with reference to the *Sruti*, the perception of the reflected object is of an illusive nature. It is the conclusion of another class of thinkers that the *Sruti* is the cause of the note, in the same sense that a lump of clay is the cause of an earthen-pot. But this kind of reasoning is faulty too, inasmuch as the clay may be distinguished in the presence of the earthen-pot, whereas the *Sruti* cannot be perceived in the presence of the note. Some other thinkers make out that the *Sruti* is transformed into a note in the manner in which milk is transformed to curd. There seems to be some force in this simile.

From the Table given, it would appear that there are four *Srutis* respectively in *Sharja* (C), *Madhyama* (F), and *Panchama* (G); three, in *Rishabha* (D) and *Dhaivata* (A) respectively; and two in *Gándhára* (E) and *Nisháda* (B) respectively. According to modern use, in conformity with which the Table has been drawn up, there are three *Srutis* between *Sharja* and *Rishabha*. Hence, if *Rishabha* is lowered by one *Sruti*, it is called **Sámánya*

*It would, perhaps, be necessary to explain the Sanskrit adjuncts by which the notes raised or lowered in value are distinguished. *Komala* means *Flat*; *Tivra*=*sharp*; *Sámánya*=*slightly*; *Madhya*=*medium*: *Ati*=*very*. Thus: *Sámánya Komala Rishabha* would

Komala; if it is lowered by two *Srutis*, it is called *Madhya Komala*; and if by three, it is called *Ati Komala Rishabha*.

There are two *Srutis* between *Rishabha* and *Gándhára*. Hence *Gándhára* is called *Madhya Komala* if it is lowered by one *Sruti*; and *Ati Komala*, if it is lowered by two.

There is only one *Sruti* between *Gándhára* and *Madhyama*. But, according to uságe, the latter is never lowered. It is raised, *i. e.*, it is made sharp.

...ean *Rishabha* rendered *slightly flat*. *Ati Komala Rishabha*,—*Rishabha* rendered *very flat*; *Madhya Komala Rishabha*—*Rishabha* rendered *neither slightly flat nor very flat*.

The number of *Srutis* between *Madhyama* and *Panchama* is three. Hence, if *Madhyama* is raised by one *Sruti*, it becomes *Sámánya Tívra*; if it is raised by two *Srutis*, it becomes *Madhya Tívra*, and, if by three, it becomes *Ati Tívra.*

According to the Theory of Hindu Music, *Panchama* cannot be rendered either flat or sharp. But that makes no difference as to the pitch of the note sought to be produced; for *Madhyama* sharp amounts to the same thing as *Panchama* flat. There are three *Srutis* between *Panchama* and *Dhaivata.* If the latter is lowered by one *Sruti*, it becomes *Sámánya Komala*, if it is lowered by two *Srutis*, it becomes *Madhya Komala*, and if by three, it becomes *Ati Komala*.

Two *Srutis* lie between *Dhaivata* and *Nishdda*. Hence, if the latter is lowered by one *Sruti*, it becomes *Madhya Komala*, and if by two *Srutis*, it becomes *Ati Komala*.

The tonic (*Sharja*) C, according to Indian Music, admits of no change in its value. Its position is a fixed one.

Now, comes the question as to the values of the *Srutis*. As would appear from the Table given, the nine intervals between C and F are equal to one another, and the thirteen between F and C (*Higher*) are also equal to one another. But the intervals in the latter group are not the same as those in the former, but are rather closer to one other; for there are nine intervals in the first-half of the division, and thirteen in the second-half of it. Hence the value of the *Sruti* immediately succeeding the note F is comparatively higher than that of the one immediately preceding the same note. The intervals in the two groups are *almost* equal to one another, so far as each group is concerned—we say *almost*, because the notes arranged according to the intervals laid down do not, in some cases, form *very* accurate representations of the Diapason. But the difference is so minute as to defy detection by the ordinary ear.

To represent, as correctly as possible, the sound of the twenty-two *Srutis*, we have devised a musical instrument called *Sruti-Viṉá*, which is a *Setár* arranged with frets representing each interval of the middle octave, and mounted with strings. This instrument might give the curious some idea of the arrangement of the *Srutis* in the Diapason, and of the variety of sounds an Indian octave is credited with producing.

We have also had constructed to our order tuning forks forming a series of twenty-three (including the Tonic of the next higher octave), which, it is hoped, will give the uninitiated some idea of the *Sruti* which seems to be as much puzzle to lovers and cultivators of European Music as it is a peculiar characteristic of our own.

The *Srutis* are, as it were, the life and soul of Hindu Music. It is they that form the foundation of the natural and the chromatic intervals and the fountain-head of the various *Rágas* and *Rágiṇis* which owe their origin to the different permutations of the intervals. Attempts at harmonising Hindu Music should be made with an eye to the positions of these minute intervals. This subject has been dealt with in detail in the work,* "The Musical Scales of the Hindus," to which the attention of the interested reader is humbly invited.

* By the Author.

CONCLUDING REMARKS.

THE "*Sruti*" is known among the modern musicians of India by the name of "*Sorut.*" But I doubt whether all of them understand what is meant by that term. In the course of the general change which followed the transfer of Hindusthan from the hands of the Hindus to those of the Mahomedans, the *S'ástras* of the Hindus, including that of Music, sank into oblivion. The Mahomedan rulers encouraged the practice of Hindu Music and converted it into an instrument of sensual enjoyment. They did not at all care for the essential principles of Music which, to them, appeared uninviting and inaccessible. The consequence was that the musical *S'ástras* well nigh fell into disuse. One or two Sanskrit works on Music were translated, for the first time into Persian, by Amir Khusroo during the reign of the Pathan king Gias-uddin Balban, who ascended the throne in 1256 after Christ. Mirza Khan of Persia wrote also in Persian a musical treatise which goes by the name of "*Toftel Hind.*" The book does not show when or in whose reign it was got up. A few other Persian translations of Sanskrit works on Music are noticed, but in none of them has the subject of *Sruti* been clearly dealt with, in its theoretical or practical aspect. The Mahomedan musicians, when questioned on this subject, are generally able to say this much only that there is such a thing as *Sorut*, the nature of which, they add, it is difficult to determine. A few musical works have lately been translated into Hindi under the patronage of some of the Hindu Chiefs of the present day, but these works, too, do not give any authoritative exposition of the subject. I have known of the existence of a few Guzerati works on Hindu Music in the Presidency of Bombay, but as, unfortunately, I have not had the opportunity of making myself acquainted with their contents, I am not in a position to say whether or how they have treated the question of the *Sruti*. From the conversation I have had with a few of the musicians of Guzerat, it did not appear to me clear that they could throw any light on the subject. The Southern portion of India did not suffer so much from the influences of the Mahomedan conquests as the Northern one, and, for this reason, several Sanskrit works on Music are still extant in the Southern Presidency. The Tamil works written on the basis of the *S'ástras* deal with *Srutis* in a comparatively comprehensive manner, but it is doubtful whether the subject has been successfully treated in its *practical* view. The principles of melody, measure and of the Drama, as followed up to this day in the Southern Presidency, are exactly the same as those laid down in the classical authorities. From the work which is being published by Lieutenant C. R. Day, of the Madras Army, on the subject of Hindu Music as described in the Sanskrit works, extant in the Southern Presidency, it would appear how very different now is the Music of India to what it was before. I have had the pleasure of cultivating the acquaintance of several musicians of note hailing from the South, and can well testify to the excellence of the manner in which they have practically explained the principles of the *Rágas* in accordance with the *dicta* of the *S'ástras*. The Music of Bengal and the North-West has partaken largely of the Mahomedan element. About 50 years ago, a Bengali gentleman of the name of Babu Radha Mohun Sen of Calcutta wrote in Bengali a treatise on Music which appears to have had the "*Toftel Hind*" for its model. This is believed to be the first work on Music written in the Bengali language. The work does not speak of *Srutis* according to the views of the *S'ástras*. The author simply says that the *Srutis* are the wives of the notes; and he illustrates the metaphor by remarking that, like the wives gifted with the bashfulness natural to their sex, the *Srutis* seek protection in the persons of their husbands. This, no doubt, is poetical sentiment which throws little light on the views of the musical *S'ástras*. About seventeen years ago, my revered teacher the late Professor Kshetra Mohun Gosvami succintly stated the principles of the *Sruti* as enunciated in the ancient works, in the course of his musical work designated "*Sangíta-Sára.*" The opinions expressed on the subject by eminent Europeans versed in Hindu Music such as Sir William Jones, Capt. Willard, and others (notably among whom is Paterson who has written a lengthy dissertation on the topic), will be found collected in my publication called "Hindu Music from various Authors."

It is known to all musicians of Europe that the practice of dividing the notes into minute intervals is not confined to the Music of India. That the ancient Greeks had it will appear clear from the following passage under the heading of "Enharmonic Scale" in Nathan's work "*Musurgia Vocalis*" :—

"Enharmonic, extremely musical, so called from its superior excellence. Aristoxenus ascribes the invention of this genus to Olympus. The diastema* of the Enharmonic, according to Euclid, are two dieses and the ditonus. Brossard says, it is a species of Music, the modulation whereof proceeds by intervals less than quarter-tones. This genus was in great use among the Greeks, especially in their dramatic performances; but in what its excellences consisted we have never been able to find out. It was allowed by all to be so difficult that few could ever practise it; one of the Enharmonic scales in the time of Aristoxenus, consisted of quarter-tones and major thirds: they had originally another kind of enharmonic, which was considered much easier of execution, but is now lost."

* Diastema, an interval, or space.

Dr. Burney says:—"From several passages in ancient authors who have written upon Music, it appears that there were two kinds of *enharmonic* melodies in use among the Greeks; in the most ancient of which we do not find that the *Diesis* or *quarter-tone* ever had admission. This I shall distinguish, in the course of the following essay, by the title of *Old Enharmonic.* The other, in which the semi-tone was divided, and which seems to have been a refinement upon this, I shall call *New Enharmonic.*"

The practice still obtains among the Arabs, as would appear from the following remarks taken from Nathan:—

"Aristotle speaks of enharmonic melodies being formerly preferred to all others for their ease and simplicity. The enharmonic was in its decline in the time of Aristoxenus and the chromatic daily increasing in public favor. Dr. Burney tells us, that Dr. Russell procured him from Aleppo the Arabian scale of Music, the octave of which consisted of twenty-four quarter-tones, all of which had their particular denominations."

In his work entitled "An Introduction to the Study of National Music," Carl Engel reproduces a song of the natives of Nukahiva, (the principal Island of the Marquesas Archipelago) which illustrates the use of the quarter-tones, and remarks that it is also discernable in the vocal performances of some other barbarous nations. The New Zealanders, or Maories are reported "to be gifted with a remarkably fine ear for distinguishing quarter-tones." "Mr. Davies," adds Carl Engel, "has written a small essay, the purport of which is to prove that the succession of intervals employed by the Maories bears a close resemblance to the *enharmonic genus* of the ancient Greeks, which consisted of a succession of a quarter-tone, another quarter-tone and a major third."

The preceding pages represent a brief *resumé* of the views of classical authorities, such as Bharata, Nárada, Sárangdeva, &c., on the subject of the *Srutis*, and are written on the basis of those authorities. As would appear from the context, attempts have been made to illustrate the subject, firstly, with the help of a *Setár* in which the frets have been arranged with reference to the positions of the *Srutis* in a Diapason, and secondly, with the help of a set of tuning forks representing the intervals of the Diapason. For the idea of the latter I am indebted to Mr. A. J. Ellis, the eminent authority on Mathematical Music, at whose instance the Government of India has done me the honor of asking whether I could undertake to carry out the suggestion. The immediate object of the publication of this hurried and necessarily imperfect pamphlet will be found in the correspondence published in the Appendix. If by the construction of the tuning forks, supplemented by this brochure, I am found, even to the slightest extent, to have succeeded in carrying out the orders of the Government of India and in giving the visitors of the "Indo-Colonial Exhibition," and the European public generally, an idea of the nature and uses of the *Sruti*, my labors in this connection will have been amply recompensed. In conclusion, I think it but just to state, that my eldest son, Kumar Pramod Kumar Tagore, has considerably lessened my labors by himself undertaking to transcribe the *Srutis* on the tuning forks. My acknowledgements are also due to Mr. S. Harraden of this city, for the favor he has done me by obtaining for me such a large number of tuning forks.

CALCUTTA,
March 1886. } S. M. TAGORE.

APPENDIX.

No. $\frac{3573}{1225}$ Ex.

FROM

C. S. BAYLEY, ESQ., C. S.,

Under-Secretary to the Government of India.

TO

RAJAH SIR SOURINDRO MOHUN TAGORE,

KT., C. I. E.,

Calcutta, the 29th December 1885.

Revenue and Agricultural Department. (Exhibition).

SIR,

I AM desired to forward for your information the enclosed papers on the subject of the preparation of a set of tuning forks representing the division of the Indian octave for the forthcoming Colonial and Indian Exhibion.

Copy of letter, dated 10th November 1885, from Mr. Ellis to the Royal Commissioners for the Colonial and Indian Exhibition. Extract paragraphs 3, 4 and 5 of letter dated 23rd November 1885 from Mr. Ellis.

2. The Government of India is itself unable to provide this exhibit, but aware of the interest

taken by you in the subject of Indian Music and of your intention to send a selection of native musical instruments to the Exhibition, has directed me to forward the communications received from Mr. Ellis and to enquire whether you would wish to carry out his suggestion.

I have the honor to be
Sir,
Your most obdt. Servant,
(Sd.) CHAS. S. BAYLEY,
Under-Secretary to the Government of India.

25, ARGYLE ROAD,
KENSINGTON, LONDON, W.

23rd *November*, 1885.

To

E. C. BUCK, Esq.,
Secretary to the Government of India,
Revenue and Agricultural Department.

SIR,

3. THE music of India is very remarkable and its musical Scale has never been satisfactorily solved. It consists of a division of the octave

into 22 *Srutis*, presumed to be unequal, but no representation of these *Srutis* by *fixed tones* has ever been made.

4. My suggestion is that 23 tuning forks be procured and exhibited, giving the 22 notes of the Scale and the octave of the lowest note and hence the 22 *Srutis'* intervals. On such forks being exhibited, I undertake gratuitously to determine the exact pitch of each, as I am the only person, I believe, in England who possesses the necessary means.

5. The proper person to determine whether such forks are correctly tuned and to superintend their construction is *Rajah Comm. Sourindro Mohun Tagore*, Musical Doctor, Companion of the Order of the Indian Empire, Founder and President of the Bengal Academy of Music, Author of "The Musical Scales of the Hindus," Pathuriaghatta Rajbati, Calcutta. My suggestion is therefore that you should request him to procure such a set of forks for exhibition. He is fully aware of their value and importance to Indian music, and that they alone (to use his own words addressed to me on 22nd September, 1885) "are

calculated to bring the vexed question to a definite head."

Respectfully yours,

(Sd.) A. J. ELLIS.

(True Extract.)

(Sd.) G. A. ANDREWS,

Registrar, Revenue and Agricultural Department.

Copy of a letter from Alexander J. Ellis, Esq., F. R. S., F. S. A. Member of the Music Committee of the Inventions, Exhibitions, &c., &c., to Sir Philip Cunliffe-Owen, K. C. M. G., London, 10th November, 1885.

DEAR SIR,

ASSUMING that it is intended to illustrate fully the remarkable Music of India at the Indian and Colonial Exhibition 1886, I beg respectfully to suggest through you to the Royal Commission, that any exhibit will be incomplete, unless means are taken to determine the complete Indian division of the octave into *Srutis,* presumed to be unequal, and that the only certain means of doing so is to cause 23 forks to be tuned to the Indian middle *Saptaka* or septime, the intermediate tones and the octave of the lowest note.

Also I would suggest that the only person in India fit to superintend such a set of forks and pronounce that they are correct, is Rajah Sourindro Mohun Tagore, Musical Doctor, Companion of the Order of the Indian Empire, Founder and President of the Bengal Academy of Music, Calcutta, Author of the "Musical Scales of the Hindus," 1884. I therefore respectfully suggest that the Rajah be requested to furnish such a set of forks for the Exhibition.

If such forks arrive in England, I will gratuitously examine them, and furnish the number of vibrations of each fork, as I am perhaps the only man in England who possesses the necessary instruments. By this means the Indian Musical Scale which has long been a vexed question will be known accurately for the very first time.

I, therefore, finally suggest that this is an opportunity not to be neglected.

Be kind enough to bring this letter to the notice of the Royal Commission.

Forwarded to the Secretary to the Government of India, Revenue and Agricultural Department, for his consideration. Mr. Ellis has also been recommended to apply to India direct on the subject of his letters.

(Sd.) J. R. ROYLE.
